The Vatican

The Vatican

photographed by Fred Mayer

texts by Peter Hebblethwaite
Hanno Helbling
Victor J. Willi
Peter Nichols
D. Redig de Campos
Raimondo Manzini

The Vendome Press

Photo Captions

1 The Vatican City lies to the west of the old centre of Rome, on the right bank of the Tiber. Its total area, which is all but completely surrounded by protective walls, covers only 108.5 acres. Just over one half of its 750 or so inhabitants are also Vatican citizens. Altogether approximately 3,000 people are employed in the administration and management of the state. The ground plan of the whole area resembles a trapezoid, half of which is covered by buildings (containing something in the region of 11,000 rooms), squares and streets; the Vatican Gardens make up the other half.

2 Saint Peter's Square, built in the seventeenth century by the architect and sculptor Giovanni Lorenzo Bernini on the commission of Pope Alexander VII, is one of the sights of Rome. Here, the Hungarian artist, Koos Huvas Gergély from Budapest, well known for his paintings of European squares and palaces, tries to match his talent with Saint Peter's Basilica and Bernini's colonnades.

3 Michelangelo's cupola rises directly above the Apostle's tomb and the high altar, and is the focal point of Saint Peter's. From beneath, however, it is somewhat upstaged by the gigantic canopy built by Bernini in the reign of Pope Sixtus V. Eighty-eight feet high, the gold-bronze canopy is the same height as the Palazzo Farnese. The cupola is 400 feet in height, including tambour; encircling its inner circumference, a sight-seers' gallery, 220 feet up, gives a spectacular view of the basilica interior.

4 Just a few days after his election, Pope John Paul II unexpectedly leaves the Vatican to visit his old friend from Poland, Bishop Andrea Deskur, seriously ill in the Gemelli Clinic. With this gesture, the new Pope shows his readiness to make spontaneous decisions with little regard for bureaucratic protocol. Romans lining the street greet their new Pontiff with delight. For the first time in 450 years, the Pope is a non-Italian.

5 On important feast-days, up to 200,000 people can gather in Saint Peter's Square. Here, over 30,000 American Catholics have come for the canonisation of John Neumann, the former bishop of Philadelphia. Perched on the press platform behind the colossal statue of Saint Peter, photographers with telephoto lenses capture the moving scene on the square.

Published by The Vendome Press
Distributed in the United States of America by
The Viking Press, 625 Madison Avenue, New York, N.Y. 10022
Distributed in Canada by Penguin Books Canada Limited.
© Orell Füssli Verlag Zürich 1979.
English texts and translations:
© Gill and Macmillan Ltd and The Vendome Press 1980
Library of Congress Cataloging in Publication Data
Main entry under title:
The Vatican.
   Translation of Vatikan.
   1. Vatican City—Description—Views. 2. Catholic Church—
Pictorial Works. I. Mayer, Fred, 1933 . II. Hebblethwaite, Peter.
DG792.5.V3713   945'.634   80–50854
ISBN 0-86565-002-0

Printed and bound in Switzerland.

Contents

The Vatican and Its Organization

Peter Hebblethwaite

Vatican is one of those words—like Kremlin and Pentagon—which carries an aura of power and mystery. Of course it cannot compete with the two newcomers when one looks at the balance of world forces in purely material terms. But the Vatican is precisely the joker in the international pack. The Papacy antedates every known political institution in the world. It is a pocket-handkerchief state, smaller than Saint James's Park, and yet its absolute sovereign, the Pope, has an authority that is unique in the world. He has, as Stalin scoffed, no divisions. But he has something else more fundamental: spiritual power. The reality of this elusive concept of 'spiritual power' was tested in June 1979 when Pope John Paul II went back home to his native Poland. The Polish government and its 'friendly ally', the Soviet Union, had all the physical power needed to prevent John Paul II from making a journey that they cannot have welcomed; and yet they could not keep him out without provoking an international furore that they preferred not to risk. He went to Poland.

But though the phrase 'spiritual power' conveys something real, it is also a puzzling and paradoxical expression. For the Church of Christ is not based on power at all. It was based from the outset on the experience of the Cross—and that was in the first instance an experience of failure. The Cross was, and remains, 'a folly to the Greeks and scandal to the Jews', where the 'Greeks' stand for all those whose criteria are purely humanist and this-worldly and the 'Jews' for all those whose religion does not admit of the experience of the radically new. Modern exegetes prefer not to speak of the 'foundation' of the Church, as though there were an analogy between Jesus setting up the Church and, say, Karl Marx establishing the Communist Party. They prefer to say that the Church comes into being as the response of a group of first-century Jews and then Gentiles to the life and message of Jesus. Tragedy and death were banal in the ancient world. John the Baptist was beheaded and Spartacus was crucified. Both had followers, but they were quickly dispersed and forgotten. Jesus also was crucified. But his followers did not take that as the final word. They believed that God had raised him up, that the new era of the Spirit was inaugurated in Jesus, and that they were the new and definitive 'People of God' with a mission to the whole world.

Because they formed a 'people', and not just a disorganised rabble, the early Christians had a concept of Church order. Peter had been given the task of 'confirming the faith of the brethren'. He was the rock-apostle. But part of the originality of Christianity was that it had a new idea of how to exercise authority which rejected secular models: 'The kings of the Gentiles exercise lordship over them, and those in authority are called benefactors. But not so with you; rather let the greatest among you become as the youngest, and the leader as one who serves' (Luke 22: 25–26). It is this principle, often obscured, that permits us to speak today of the 'spiritual power' of the Vatican. Though in its twenty centuries of history the Papacy has not always followed this maxim, and at times has betrayed it or made a mockery of it, the idea that the papal ministry, like all ministry in the Church, is for service, not domination, has been the thread which has linked the Church to the New Testament.

It is, of course, erroneous to use the terms 'Vatican' and 'Papacy' interchangeably. Throughout most of the first millenium, after the conversion of the Emperor Constantine (usually dated 312), the Popes

5

lived and worked in the Lateran Palace. That is why the basilica of Saint John Lateran remains to this day 'the Pope's cathedral' and why it is known as 'the head and mother of all churches'. Pope Gregory the Great (590–604), the first Pope to use the title 'servant of the servants of God', imposed a pattern that became dominant in the Middle Ages and can still be detected today: the Lateran was a monastic enclave, and therefore predominantly male and celibate. Between 350 and 1347, no one could have said 'the Vatican' meaning 'the Papacy'. In that sense the Vatican is a modern institution.

But even so the Christians of the first millenium knew about the Vatican Hill. In Roman times it had been unhealthy and despised, a place of swamps and mosquitoes and snakes, with just a few herdsmen tending their ragged sheep. It became a Christian shrine because it was believed that Saint Peter was buried there. The Vatican rests, literally and metaphorically, on the bones of Peter. That he came to Rome, centre of the Empire, and was crucified there, is well attested. But where are his remains?

In the middle of Saint Peter's Square there stands an obelisk. It was placed there in 1586 by order of Pope Sixtus V. It took 900 men and 400 horses to transport it from its previous site—on the left of Saint Peter's about where the sacristy now stands—and they nearly met with disaster. When the huge stone was almost in position, it swayed ominously and it seemed that the ropes were about to give way. The situation was saved by a Genoese sailor who cried out in dialect, 'Water on the ropes, water on the ropes'. His nautical experience told him this would tighten them. The obelisk is mute. But if it could speak, it could tell us why the Vatican is where it is.

The obelisk was brought from Egypt in the reign of the Emperor Caligula in what Pliny says was the most splendid ship anyone had yet seen. It was set up, in accordance with custom, to mark the middle of the private circus that Caligula and then Nero were building across the Tiber. The circus was between the Gianiculum Hill to the south and the Vatican Hill to the north. (Nervi's new Audience Hall probably covers part of its site.) There were other and more famous circuses on the other side of the Tiber. But in the year A.D. 64 they had all been put out of action by the disastrous fire which swept through the mainly wooden city on the night of 18–19 July. It raged on for nine more days. The Emperor Nero, who had not been fiddling but had been at the seaside, immediately set about grandiose architectural projects for a new Rome with such enthusiasm that many Romans, foodless and homeless, suspected him of having had the fire started himself to make possible his dreams of urban reconstruction. It was to distract the populace and to scotch such rumours that Nero organised the games in his newly completed circus for 13 October. It was the anniversary of the day on which he became Emperor. He hoped to entertain the people and at the same time to pin the blame for the fire on the obscure sect from Palestine who were already known as Christians or 'followers of the way'.

The obelisk was the witness of what happened next and Tacitus has recorded the details. The Emperor himself took part in the games and drove a wildly careering chariot round the three hundred metre track. A large number of Christians were put to death by three different methods. Some were dressed in animal skins, and then torn to pieces by wild beasts, a method of execution that left no remains. Others became human torches to light up the October sky and to warm the spectators—for Roman nights in October can be chilly. Once again, there would be no remains. Yet others were crucified, for at festivals such as this, executions often became the high point of the entertainment. Ghastly though crucifixion was as a form of execution, at least it left the broken body to be collected; and the Romans, though indifferent to life, were superstitiously reverent of the dead. If the obelisk could speak, it would tell us whether Peter was crucified upside down, as legend says. But that he was crucified in Nero's circus on 13 October A.D. 64 is highly probable.

Disposing of the body would have been the least of problems. The Vatican Hill was already the site of numerous tombs, starting from the splendid monument to Hadrian down by the Tiber (now known as the Castel San Angelo) and moving along the Via Cornelia towards more modest graves. Towards the top of the desolate hill it would have been easy to place the remains of Peter into a crevice among the rocks and cover them with a stone. The exact spot would have been carefully marked. The place where Peter was buried became a secret Christian shrine.

Less than three hundred years later the Emperor Constantine decided to build a church over the bones of Saint Peter. To make this possible, the Vatican Hill had to be levelled down. An L-shaped segment was cut out of it, and the earth was moved from the right to the left as you look at Saint Peter's today. This explains why the papal apartments seem higher in relation to Saint Peter's than one would expect, and why the hill rises so steeply behind the church. Constantine's church, built on the basilica pattern (Santa Sabina survives to give us an idea of what it was like), lasted for over a thousand years. An Italian sixteenth-century print shows the old church and the old square (it *was* a square) with the great dome of the new church rising behind it. It was a wonder of the civilised world, and it owed its legitimacy to the presence of Peter.

It is impossible to write the Papacy's history succinctly. Where theologians see a steady development, under the guidance of the Holy Spirit, historians see rather a complex pattern of response to challenges and almost accidental progress. Perhaps the two points of view are not totally opposed. Obliged to be brief, we can put on seven-league boots and march rapidly down the centuries, picking out some of the key turning points.

Constantine did more than build the first Saint Peter's. By the Edict of Milan in 313 all laws prejudicial to Christians were abolished and the members of the once persecuted sect were now allowed to form legal corporations. Church and Empire buttressed each other—though there were often tensions. In 389 the Emperor Theodosius went further and made Christianity the official creed of the Empire. By now the seat of the Empire had been transferred to Constantinople, and this paved the way for the emergence of the Popes as both the temporal and spiritual rulers of the West. For the Emperors were far away, often involved in endless hair-splitting theological disputes, preoccupied with the defence of the eastern frontiers, as a consequence of which they could not keep effective control in the West. The Popes filled the power vacuum.

In 754 Pope Stephen II (752–757) became the first Pope to cross the Alps (Popes had travelled before, but to the East, sometimes in chains). He went to beg the aid of Pepin III, King of the Franks, against the marauding Lombards. A deal was struck. Pepin overcame the Lombards and in a treaty known as the 'Donation of Pepin' handed over some captured cities to the Pope. This was the basis of the temporal power of the Papacy which lasted until 1870. Significantly the keys of the captured cities were laid on the tomb of Saint Peter. They were assigned to 'Saint Peter and the Roman Church', two inseparable concepts.

In the tenth century, however, the Papacy was at its lowest ebb. Popes rarely died peacefully in their beds. One was strangled (Stephen VI in 896), another was smothered (Benedict VI in 974), while John XII, whose diversions included incest and satanism, died in the arms of his mistress. It took a very tough-minded Pope to begin to restore order or even propriety. Gregory VII (surnamed Hildebrand) inaugurated a period of reform which had three main concerns: to restore the lost authority and prestige of the Papacy—in the name of Saint Peter; to denounce and if possible root out clerical corruption, especially simony and unchastity; and to assert the power of the Church over feudal lords, princes and emperors who would no longer be allowed to appoint bishops and abbots. This was the quarrel about 'investiture'. It was concluded with the famous occasion, one winter's day in 1077 at Canossa, when the repentant and humiliated Emperor Henry IV knelt in the snow to receive the Pope's absolution.

But by the fourteenth century, the Church was internally divided, with Popes and anti-popes in Avignon staking out their rival claims. Saints were confused as well. Each Pope had his Curia and his supporters. Just to compound the confusion, a third claimant appeared on the scene. The dispute and the scandal of a three-headed Papacy were only resolved at the Council of Constance which took place in the years 1414–18. The fact that it took a Council to restore some dignity to the Papacy is not without theological significance.

Crisis succeeded crisis. The Church in the sixteenth century was guilty of worldliness in high places, corruption and venality. But the Popes were also patrons of the arts, and set about rebuilding Rome. They were hardly in a position to withstand the shock of the Reformation, although there were Catholic reformers who read the signs of the times correctly. The ill-fated Dutch Pope, Adrian VI, (the last non-Italian before John Paul II) reigned for just over a year (1522–23). He wrote: 'We, prelates and clergy, have gone astray from the right path, and for a long time there is none that has done good, no, no one. . . . Therefore we promise that we will use all diligence to reform before all else the Roman Curia whence, perhaps, all these evils have their origin.' He died before he could set about the work of reform.

But that is one of the 'maybes' of history. The response of the Popes to the Reformation that actually happened was the Council of Trent (1545–63). From many points of view, it can be considered a reforming council which set the pattern for priestly and episcopal life almost down to the present. But its debates were conducted in a polemical atmosphere in which it was impossible to be fair to the Protestants, and any hint of possible convergence was instantly rejected for fear of contamination. Thus Trent also proved unable to do justice to balanced Catholic positions. If the Protestants rejected auricular confession—then confession must be made the basis of the spiritual life. If they rejected prayers to the saints—then the saints must be honoured in ever more splendid statuary and reliquaries.

It is this Counter-Reformation spirit which most marks the art and architecture of the Vatican today. The city of Rome is a baroque city, not a Renaissance city like Florence. It is full of display, ostentation, *trompe l'œil*, fountains, façades like stage-sets. As H.V. Morton said, the saints on the portico of Saint Peter's seem to be crying out, 'We've got it in the bag'. There was a confidence, a swagger, an arrogance about the Counter-Reformation that is reflected in the new Saint Peter's. There was also a more spiritual side to the Counter-Reformation that could be seen in the mettlesome saints that it produced—men like Ignatius of Loyola and Philip Neri and mystical women like Teresa of Avila (her swooning statue by Bernini has often been thought to sum up the baroque temper). It was in this period that the Roman Curia began to take on the shape which it still has today: it ceased to be merely a 'court' (like a royal court) and became more of an effective bureaucracy and administration. In 1588 Sixtus V gave it a coherent and functional organisation. In the map rooms an immense missionary effort in Latin America and the Far East was plotted and monitored. From now on people began to speak of 'the Vatican' in the modern sense.

This became even truer after the First Vatican Council (1869–70) which completed the centralisation of the Church begun by Trent. It defined papal primacy and papal infallibility in such a way that some enthusiasts declared that there would never be any need for a subsequent council. Recent historians have suggested that the minority opposition at Vatican I was not entirely free, and that its sound arguments were suppressed or circumvented. 'I am tradition', Pius IX is reliably reported to have said. In his vision of the world the Church was necessarily in opposition to the main trends of the nineteenth century. He denounced secularism, liberalism, socialism and communism. New means of communication meant that every allocution of the Pope could be flashed round the world and Catholics were expected to benefit from the ordinary (or everyday) *magisterium*. The Church became more Rome-centred than ever before. National colleges expanded, and the first rung on the ecclesiastical ladder was to have studied in one of them.

The paradox was that this supreme assertion of the authority of the Papacy came at the very moment when all temporal power was lost. In September 1870 Italian troops invaded Rome, and the city was completely occupied a month later. The Pope retreated into the Vatican, refused to have any dealings with the Italian monarchy, forbade Catholics to enter political life, and thought of himself as 'the prisoner of the Vatican'. It was this way of thinking which led later Popes, like Pius XI, to appear at their study windows on Sunday mornings to say the Angelus and bless the crowds: the Pope could not go to the people, so they would have to come to him, trapped in his fourth-floor room. The custom survived even after the Lateran Treaty of 11 February 1929, signed with Mussolini. The Lateran Treaty resolved the 'Roman Question', gave the Vatican certain extra-territorial rights in Rome and at Castelgandolfo, provided funds in compensation for the loss of the Papal States which, on the whole wisely invested, have been the basis of Vatican financial prosperity ever since. It was only in the late 1970s, with mounting inflation, that the financial alarm bells began to sound. The Lateran Treaty also resulted in the building of the Via della Conciliazione, the avenue which leads up to Saint Peter's from the Tiber. It makes a splendid vista and a splendid approach, but some have regretted that the area around the Vatican—apart from the Borgo Pio on the right—is now practically uninhabited, except by religious orders.

The Second Vatican Council (1962–65) was the final stage in the development of the modern Papacy. It was summoned by John XXIII, elected as a 'stop-gap' Pope. But he astonished the world, and made the word *charisma* come alive again in its appropriate context of faith. Vatican I had not said the last word, after all, and Vatican II corrected many of its emphases. One of Pope John's reasons for summoning another council was that he wanted to make available to the whole Church the best insights of its different parts. He had seen in his own experience the harm done by the repression of theologians and excessive centralisation. He did not pretend to be omnicompetent but preferred to be an 'enabler'. The council was called to permit the bishops to face their responsibilities for the whole Church ('collegiality'), to return to the sources of the Church's self-understanding ('History will be our teacher', he said), to rethink the relationship of Church and world, to exchange the notion of domination for that of service, to extend a brotherly hand to all who shared in the name of Christian, and to open up a dialogue with all men of good will. John XXIII even had a good word for communists who, despite their errors, had not forfeited their human rights and could still have doctrines that contained 'good and useful elements'. It was a vast programme, and those who called it 'revolutionary' were not entirely wrong.

Pope John died on Whit Monday, 1963, after only one session of the council. So the working out of these ideas was left to his successor, Pope Paul VI. He was an anguished and scrupulous intellectual, a man with a keen sense of nuance and precedent. He could not reproduce the *charisma* of John XXIII but he did not wish to emulate the autocratic ways of Pius XII. Sometimes this resulted in 'dithering', but when he made up his mind and settled questions on his own—priestly celibacy and artificial contraception are the obvious examples—the world did not exactly praise him for his remarkable courage.

Yet his achievements were considerable. He steered the council through three more sessions to a harmonious conclusion. He took care to respect the minority at the council without being bullied by it. He committed himself personally to the implementation of the council decrees and made liturgical reform and ecumenism an integral part of Catholicism. He set about the reform of the Roman Curia. It was to be internationalised, modern languages would be used henceforward, top offices had to be reviewed every five years, and on the death of a Pope all the prefects of Roman Congregations would automatically resign so as to give the new Pope a free hand. Most important of all, as an old Curia hand who knew the ins and outs of the Vatican, he tried to bring the various congregations (they would be called 'ministries' in a secular government) under control by giving the Secretariat of State a 'co-ordinating' function. This led to further accusations of centralisation, especially after 1967 when the energetic, tireless Monsignor Giovanni Benelli became *sostituto* (second-in-command) at the Secretariat of State. He mastered the briefs, supervised the personnel, made things hum. This aroused resentment in those accustomed to working at a slower pace. But without some such centralisation it seems likely that the Roman Curia could not have been induced to take seriously the implementation of Vatican II.

Paul VI also created new bodies to enable the voice of the local Churches to be heard in the Vatican. The most important was the advisory body known as the Synod of Bishops. It could act as a counterweight to the Roman Curia. In 1969, as a result of a suggestion by the Synod, he set up the International Theological Commission, a body of thirty eminent theologians from all over the world, whose advice would be more broadly-based than that offered by the Roman theologians who worked in the Congregation for the Doctrine of Faith. Finally, Paul VI transformed the College of Cardinals, the body which would elect his successor. On his death on 6 August 1978, 111 cardinals went to the

Vatican for the conclave. One can measure how far he had internationalised the college by comparing the regional origins of the cardinals in 1978 with the situation in 1963. In 1978 there were fifty-six from Europe, including twenty-seven Italians; twelve from Africa (compared with two in 1963); nineteen Latin Americans (eleven in 1963); thirteen from Asia and Oceania (five in 1963); and eleven North Americans (seven in 1963). The likelihood of there being a non-Italian Pope was increased.

After the interlude of the 'smiling Pope', John Paul I, that is precisely what happened. The cardinals surprised the waiting world—and possibly themselves as well—by electing the first non-Italian for 455 years, the first Pope in his fifties for over a hundred years, and the first Slav Pope ever: Karol Wojtyla. This is not the place to provide an assessment of his pontificate, though some hints will appear in the description of the way the Roman Curia is working at present. In the long march of the Papacy through history, the important point is that the two John Pauls between them restored the original link with the tomb of Saint Peter as the necessary basis not of their temporal power—which they do not possess in any real sense—but of their spiritual authority.

This could be seen in the way both of them, at their inauguration Masses, discarded the tiara—the symbol of regal power that can be seen all over the Vatican. It was of Asiatic origin and wholly unsuited to 'the servant of the servants of God'. (Bismarck, on hearing that it was supposed to represent authority over heaven, hell and earth, is reported to have said that he would gladly leave the first two realms to the Pope provided he could look after the third himself.) Instead, John Paul I and John Paul II received the pallium, an eminently Christian symbol. It has been presented to metropolitan archbishops, of both East and West, since the fourth century. It is made of lamb's wool, presented to the Pope on the feast of Saint Agnes: it is therefore linked with pastoral care. It is placed over the shoulders and resembles a yoke: it is a reminder that the service of unity will not be easy but that, with the help of the Lord, the burden will be light. Finally it is presented as coming from the tomb of Saint Peter: thus all stewardship in the Church is linked to the founding apostle.

Once again we are reminded that there would be nothing on the Vatican Hill, except perhaps multi-storey blocks of flats, were it not for the presence of Peter's bones. The spiritual authority of the Popes depends upon a continuity of mission. The Vatican is built on a failure, transformed by the hope of resurrection.

John Paul II received the pallium 'from the tomb of Saint Peter' on 22 October 1978. His first words on that day stressed the continuity with Peter: 'Thou art the Christ, the Son of the Living God' (Matthew 16:15). What is his inheritance and what are the means at his disposal for the service of unity which is the essence of his mission?

The first part of the answer is statistical. The Central Office of Statistics of the Vatican—a new body with a splendid computer—provides annual figures, but they are always two years out of date. Here are the latest figures. In 1977 there were 739 million baptised Roman Catholics compared with 724 million in 1976. This meant that in 1977 they made up 18.1 per cent of the estimated world population (roughly comparable to the number of Moslems and fewer than the Chinese). They lived in 2,372 dioceses which had 3,700 bishops (including auxiliaries). There were 421,859 priests, of whom 259,965 were diocesans (what used to be called secular priests) and 161,894 religious. The number of religious sisters in the world is just short of a million: 986,686.

The distribution of the world's Catholic population was as follows:
Africa: 52,508,000 or 12.4 per cent of the population;
North America: 58,349,000 or 24.3 per cent of the population;
Mainland Central America: 79,114,000 or 93.6 per cent of the population;
Central American Islands: 17,529,000 or 62.7 per cent of the population;
Latin America: 204,104,000 or 91.3 per cent of the population;
Asia: Middle East: 1,831,000 or 1.5 per cent of the population;
Asia: Far East: 54,182,000 or 2.4 per cent of the population;
Europe: 266,034,000 or 39.8 per cent of the population;
Oceania (including Australia): 5,475,000 or 25 per cent of the population.

Just as important as these figures are the trends which they indicate. The signs are that Europe and North America, which made up more than 51 per cent of the Church in 1960, are losing their dominance. By the year 2000 the projection is that they will only constitute 30 per cent of the total while the remainder will come from the 'third world'.

All of the world's 739 million Catholics are aware of the existence of the Pope. Many of them will have seen him on television, especially since 1964 when Paul VI became 'the pilgrim Pope' who travelled the world. John Paul II has shown every sign that he will be even more of a travelling Pope: in his first year of office he went to Mexico, Poland, Ireland, the United States and Turkey; and there are twenty-three invitations elsewhere on his desk that have not been formally refused. Television has made the Pope 'visible' and changed the way of exercising his office: it permits a direct relationship with many parts of the Church and so makes more real the task of embodying the unity of the whole Church. The Pope no longer thinks of himself nor acts as though he were 'the prisoner of the Vatican'.

But very few of the world's 739 million Catholics know anything at all about those who work in the Vatican—the Roman Curia. It has 3,000 members, including part-time consultants who mostly work in the five Roman universities. The two papal conclaves of 1978 turned the spotlight on the cardinal members of the Curia who hitherto had been invisible and largely unknown. The most improbable men were declared *papabili*— which merely indicated how open the field was. But once the elections were over, they returned to the obscurity from which they had been briefly snatched.

It is chiefly bishops and religious superiors who need to know the Roman Curia and how it works: they have to bear the brunt of explaining its decisions and applying them in local circumstances. Ordinary Catholics are at the end of a long chain of command. That is why it is easy and tempting to dismiss the Curia as a group of 'faceless men' sitting in marble-floored and stucco-ceilinged palaces who do not understand the pressures of everyday life in the world. This judgment is, on the whole, unfair. So in what follows an attempt will be made both to 'demythologise' the Roman Curia and to 'humanise' it.

There is no 'deputy Pope', no one who is, as in the United States' vice-presidency, 'a heart-beat away from office'. A Pope dies, and the whole procedure of electing his successor swings into play immediately. But the Pope, however, does have a second-in-command, a chief executive, who combines the functions of prime minister and foreign minister. (So long as the Papal States existed, that really was his role.) The present Secretary of State, Cardinal Agostino Casaroli, is a diplomat by training. Since 1961 when John XXIII despatched him to Vienna for a United Nations meeting on consular relations, he has been closely involved in dealing with the communist governments of Eastern Europe where there are an estimated 60 million Catholics. This experience made him congenial to Pope John Paul II, and his diplomatic acumen is also useful to a pastoral-minded and hyperactive Pope who is inclined to be as interventionist as possible. (Secretaries of State vary enormously in the responsibility given to them and what they actually do: Cardinal Jean Villot, Casaroli's predecessor, was much less interested in international affairs and made the relationships between episcopal conferences his main field of interest.) After the reform of the Roman Curia in 1967, the Secretary of State became the chief co-ordinator of the different departments. He presides at the meetings of Congregations.

He is also in effect the Prefect of the Council for the Public Affairs of the Church, the body responsible for the Vatican diplomatic service. For the existence of the Vatican City state, small as it is, permits the Church to be represented diplomatically—either by nuncios, pro-nuncios or apostolic delegates—to over a hundred countries. They do not have to be Catholic or even Christian: there are relations, for example, with the Arab countries of the Middle East and with Yugoslavia. The Vatican is also represented in international organisations such as the United Nations where the Holy See (to give it its correct title) has a permanent observer. He does not vote, but is believed to exercise hidden influence.

The Vatican diplomatic service has often been criticised. Its representatives were once said to be 'spies on the local Churches', and it is true that they play an important role in the appointment of bishops. It may seem diplomatically preferable at times to preserve the *status quo* by lending support to an unjust regime (usually a military dictatorship) rather than listen to the local bishops who denounce its tyranny. This is not an imaginary situation: it happened during the last months of the Somoza regime in Nicaragua. But despite these objections, the Vatican diplomatic service can be useful. It successfully intervened to avert war in the Beagle Straits dispute between Chile and Argentina. And Vatican diplomats can act as a buffer between the local bishops and a precarious government: if a government falls, it is easier to replace a compromised nuncio than compromised bishops.

The Secretariat of State is housed within the Apostolic Palace itself, on the floor beneath the Pope. This physical closeness is an expression of its spiritual closeness to the Pope. The remaining Vatican departments to be discussed are not, strictly speaking, in the Vatican at all. Many of them are on the Via della Conciliazione or the streets just off it, while much of the 'new', post-conciliar Curia is in the Palazzo San Callisto in Trastevere.

The eight Roman 'Congregations' are concerned with the internal life of the Church. They would be ministries or departments in a secular government. Each of them is presided over by a cardinal, known as the Prefect, and has a governing council of cardinals. Since they tend to overlap and serve on several Congregations at once, a relatively small handful of Roman cardinals can wield great authority. The fact, for instance, that cardinals 'without portfolio' like Wladislaw Rubin and Paolo Bertoli do not head Congregations does not mean that they are uninfluential.

The Congregation for the Doctrine of Faith began life in 1542 as the Congregation of the Inquisition. Later it was known as the Holy Office. It has not found it easy to live down these origins. Its primary concern was with orthodoxy and its defence in the face of Protestant onslaughts. Its most famous victim was Galileo (he got off lightly) and the most frightening was Giordano Bruno, who was burned at the stake. His statue can be seen in Campo dei Fiori. It was known, in the past, as the 'supreme' Congregation on the grounds that since doctrine was of primary importance, it could over-ride all other Congregations. It was attacked in the most vigorous terms for its defensiveness and hostility to theological research by Cardinal Joseph Frings of Cologne at the Second Vatican Council on 10 November 1963. There was widespread agreement that it was in need of reform.

On the day before the council ended, 7 December 1965, Paul VI published a *motu proprio*, *Integrae Servandae*, which began the reform of the Holy Office. Its name was to be changed to the Congregation for the Doctrine of Faith. But this constituted more than a cosmetic change: it was meant to indicate a shift in attitude. Henceforward the Congregation was to have not merely a watchdog function but the task of stimulating and promoting theological endeavour, since, said Paul VI, 'the best way to defend the faith is to encourage sound doctrine'. Heresy-hunts were to cease. Some form of dialogue—yet to be worked out—would replace inquisitorial procedures. The whole business of watching over the soundness of doctrine was to become more 'evangelical'.

Throughout the pontificate of Paul VI the Congregation for the Doctrine of Faith kept a low profile. It was not inactive, but it did not issue condemnations. It responded to Hans Küng's book, *Infallible?—An Enquiry* (1971) with a declaration called *Mysterium Ecclesiae* in which it suggested how far Catholic theologians might go in the interpretation of dogmatic statements as 'time-bound': the answer was, surprisingly far. Its declaration on sexual morality early in 1977 reasserted traditional moral teaching, but that was not a matter of surprise: no theologians were denounced by name. Only with the pontificate of John Paul II has there been a reversion to older habits. In April 1979 Father Jacques Pohier, a French Dominican, was forbidden to teach or to say Mass in public, and on 18 December of the same year the title of 'Catholic theologian' was withdrawn from Hans Küng. Meanwhile, Edward Schillebeeckx O.P. had submitted to a three-day investigation by three theologians appointed by the Congregation, and there were rumours of other investigations to come. The Congregation for the Doctrine of Faith was back in business.

The remaining Congregations can be more briefly dealt with. The Congregation of Bishops, founded in 1588, has been described as 'the ministry of the interior' of the Church. It appoints bishops (with the Pope's approval), determines the boundaries of new dioceses, and receives the five-yearly reports from bishops. The Congregation of the Clergy, set up in 1564, looks after diocesan priests. It was originally intended to oversee the implementation of the Council of Trent. It has retained something of this role in that it is also responsible for new catechisms. The Congregation for Religious and Secular Institutes explains itself. It was founded in 1601, although until Saint Pius X it remained a sub-section of the Congregation of Bishops. Its 'constituency' is made up of religious priests, brothers and nuns.

The Congregation for the Sacraments and Divine Worship is concerned with liturgical books and with liturgical reform, to the extent that it is still incomplete. It also deals with the validity of priestly ordination and with certain marriage cases (for marriages that are duly performed but non-consummated). The Congregation for the Causes of Saints prepares canonisations and beatifications, and also does the preliminary studies before someone can be declared a 'doctor' of the Church. Saint Teresa of Avila was given this title—the first woman ever— on 5 March 1970.

Two Congregations deal with 'sectors' of Church life. The Congregation for the Oriental Churches is a nineteenth-century creation, set up by Pius IX in 1862, though it only gained real independence in 1938. It covers Egypt, Eritrea, Ethiopia, Bulgaria, Cyprus, Greece, the Lebanon, Israel, Syria, Jordan and Iraq. The members of the Congregation, in addition to the cardinals named by the Pope, are the seven Oriental Patriarchs. There are more than twenty Oriental Churches. They are of immense symbolic importance in the life of the Church since they demonstrate that a great diversity of customs (including a married clergy) and liturgical rites are no obstacle to Catholic unity. But at the same time they are often under great pressure, living either under severe handicaps in the Arab or communist world or else scattered in the diaspora. There are just over 11 million Oriental Catholics.

The Congregation for the Evangelisation of Peoples (formerly known as Propaganda, until Goebbels discredited the word) was established in 1622. It is responsible for missions and for the development of new and young Churches. It co-ordinates missionary activity, encourages the development of a local clergy, and does fund-raising in the developed world. It bases itself on the premise of the conciliar decree *Ad Gentes* which reminded Catholics that 'the whole Church is missionary and that the work of evangelisation is a fundamental task of the people of God' (No. 35).

Finally the Congregation for Catholic Education deals with seminaries and institutions of higher education. Its most recent document, the apostolic constitution *Sapientia Christiana* (15 April 1979), treats every aspect of the question, including the controversial matter of the 'canonical mission' which is required of Catholic teachers of theology. But strictly speaking, the Congregation is responsible only for *pontifical* universities or faculties. Most of the universities of the United States escape its direct control. Early in 1980 Cardinal William Wakefield Baum, formerly Archbishop of Washington, was made its Prefect.

To complete this sketch of the 'old' Curia one needs to add that there are three tribunals: the Apostolic Signature, which is the supreme court of appeal; the Roman Rota—the name comes from the circular building in which its meetings were once held—which deals with difficult nullity cases; and the Apostolic Penitentiary which solves tricky cases of conscience.

All the Congregations and Tribunals so far mentioned have a long and complex history. They were all modified in various ways by Paul VI's reform of the Curia in *Regimini Ecclesiae* (15 August 1967). There were significant changes of name and a redefinition of functions. This had become necessary because of the new bodies which came into existence as a result of the Second Vatican Council. It is fair to say that while the 'old' Curia was defensive and inward-looking, the 'new' Curia was intended to embody the aspirations of the council towards dialogue and greater openness to the world.

The most important of the new bodies is the Secretariat for Christian Unity. At the council itself it was instrumental in shepherding the ecumenical 'observers' who were present, and in making sure that their concerns were not neglected. Since the council it has been responsible for dialogue with other Christian Churches—notably the dialogues with the Anglican Communion, the Lutheran World Federation and, most recently, with the thirteen Orthodox Churches, as announced by John Paul II in Constantinople on 30 November 1979. One of the great strengths of the Secretariat is that in over sixty countries there exist National Ecumenical Commissions which continue its work on the local level and can provide useful 'feed-back'. So the Secretariat for Christian Unity is the least sheltered, the best-informed and the most open-minded of curial bodies. A sub-section of the Secretariat is concerned with Jewish-Christian relations, since there is a stronger link with Judaism than with any other 'non-Christian religion'.

The two other Secretariats—for Non-Christian Religions and Non-Believers—are much smaller in size, can call upon fewer genuine experts, find it hard to engage interlocutors, and have much greater difficulty in defining precisely what their brief is. Under its much-travelled President, Cardinal Sergio Pignedoli, the Secretariat for Non-Christian Religions has striven hard to make contacts in the world of Islam as well as in those of Buddhism and Shintoism. Saffron-robed monks are not a rare sight in the Vatican. But political issues constantly impede the work and confuse the issues. The Secretariat for Non-Believers, headed by Cardinal Franz König, has held conferences on unbelief and secularisation and produced much useful documentary material; it too has local branches that have understood their task in widely differing ways. The most recent project of the Secretariat was to submit a questionnaire to scientists in order to discover the present state of the alleged conflict between science and religion. Though they may not have much to show for years of labour, these two Secretariats keep alive the essential dimension of dialogue.

It is worth noting that both the President of the Secretariat for Christian Unity (Cardinal Jan Willebrands) and the President of the Secretariat for Non-Believers (Cardinal Franz König) do not reside in Rome and have diocesan and national responsibilities in Utrecht and Vienna respectively. This is novel. It led at one time to the hope that there might be a 'decentralisation' of the Curia. But in practice the effect seems to have been to weaken the two Secretariats, who have to compete with the skilled chess players of the 'old' Curia. And it is difficult to do that if one is not on the spot all the time: *les absents ont toujours tort.* Nowhere is that principle truer than in Rome.

The Pontifical Justice and Peace Commission was set up in 1967. Paul VI compared it to a weathercock placed on the top of the Church 'as a symbol of watchfulness', and said that it would have the task of 'keeping the eye of the Church alert, her heart open and her hand outstretched for the work of love she is called upon to give to the world' (21 April 1973). It was designed to give practical expression to the Church's social concern, and to contribute towards that 'integral development' of which the encyclical *Populorum Progressio* (1967) had spoken. Like the Secretariats, it had corresponding (in both senses) national branches in many countries—though not in Eastern Europe. After a rather uneasy relationship, the national Justice and Peace Commissions secured their independence. A concern for 'justice and peace' became the Catholic euphemism for politics, and when practical political decisions were taken, often of a radical nature, the results could be divisive. They certainly alarmed the Pontifical Justice and Peace Commission which has been increasingly isolated from its own progeny and ever more integrated into the Secretariat of State which is alone competent in political and diplomatic questions on the international level. A fear of 'committing the Holy See' has inhibited its activities. The weathercock has not shown the vitality expected of it.

The Pontifical Council for the Laity was set up in response to the conciliar decree *On the Laity* (No. 26). It acquired its present title in 1976 (by analogy with the Congregations *for* Bishops and *for* Priests). Its purpose is officially stated to 'encourage the laity to take their rightful place in the Church's life and mission'. The laity, it points out with some pride, make up 98 per cent of the Church. Under its umbrella nestles the Committee for the Family.

Finally, the Pontifical Commission for the Means of Social Communication deals with the mass media (a term the Vatican prefers to avoid because people are not 'masses'). It sometimes accredits journalists and issues bulletins which tell one what will appear in the next edition of *Osservatore Romano*, the Vatican's newspaper. Close control by the Secretariat of State make it less flexible and effective than it ought to be.

What this necessarily rather dry account of the organisation of the

Roman Curia leaves out is the relative importance of the various bodies. Despite drawing-board blueprints which present a picture of harmonious collaboration and neat co-ordination, the actual relationships within the Roman Curia are constantly fluctuating. Authority—always in the end reducible to that of the Pope—shifts this way and that according to the powerful personalities in play or, though to a lesser extent, the desires of the reigning Pope. Theoretically, of course, there ought to be no problem. The Curia is at the service of the Pope and does what he says. But in practice it does not always work out like that. According to the late Cardinal Giacomo Lercaro, Pope John XXIII suffered from 'institutional solitude' in the Vatican as he struggled with entrenched ideas and vested interests inherited from the previous pontificate. His solution was to involve the Curia in the preparation of the council and then wait for the world's bishops to rend to pieces its wholly inadequate drafts. That was what happened.

Like John XXIII, John Paul II started with the initial disadvantage of being an outsider who was not very familiar with the workings of the Roman Curia. He has so far made no radical changes, and has simply filled posts as they fell vacant in a fairly conventional manner. He did not seize the chance offered him by Paul VI of starting with a completely fresh team. But already there are one or two pointers to the future.

The Congregation for the Doctrine of Faith, as we have seen, is busy with the work of scrutinising doubtful theologians. Any suggestion that the International Theological Commission could act as a counter-balance to it would be a joke in poor taste. The Secretariat for Christian Unity, on the other hand, has constantly been reminded—as though it didn't know—of the difficulties surrounding the goal of Christian unity, and of the dangers of a 'lowest common factor' solution to ecumenical divisions. This is dispiriting. Meanwhile Cardinal Sebastiano Baggio, at the Congregation of Bishops, has become a powerful figure, not least through his presidency of the Pontifical Commission for Latin America, which masterminded the Puebla meeting in February 1979 and edited its final document. Baggio also played an important role in the Special Synod of the Dutch Church held in the Vatican from 14 to 31 January 1980. The Pontifical Justice and Peace Commission is paying more attention to the theme of 'religious liberty'. At its plenary meeting in February 1980 it abandoned its scheduled debate on development to consider 'the grave threats to world peace' which put in jeopardy any work for development. In all these various ways, the Roman Curia is beginning to reflect the preoccupations of Pope John Paul II. But these trends for the most part escape all but the keenest and most dogged observers. Nevertheless they will percolate downwards and eventually affect the life of the Church.

But nothing is yet finally settled, and the reform of the Roman Curia is once again on the agenda. It was put there not by cantankerous theologians in Holland but by Pope John Paul II himself at the wholly unprecedented meeting of cardinals held in the Vatican from 4 to 8 November 1979. The meeting (it did not do to call it a 'consistory', though that was its proper name) was unprecedented because cardinals had not met as a body for over four centuries except to elect a new Pope. Here they were invited to advise the Pope on the reform of the Curia. The whole debate was conducted in the most rigorous secrecy, but from a knowledge of some of the participants it is possible to deduce that they would have stressed the following points. (1) The Roman Curia should neither be, nor be allowed to become, a 'power' within the Church, but should be 'at the service' of the Church through the intermediacy of the Pope. (2) Its serving role would be seen more clearly if it were subordinate to the *collegial* instruments which the Pope has at his disposal in the administration of the universal Church. In other words, the Curia should be subordinate to the Synod of Bishops which, at its next session in autumn 1980, is to consider 'the Roles of the Christian Family'. In addition the presence of local bishops in Curial bodies should cease to be merely a matter of 'tokenism'. (3) The most effective Curial bodies are those which, like the Secretariat for Christian Unity, are really rooted in the local Churches, and are engaged in continual and fruitful dialogue with them. This would also make clear that the Curia is not 'above' the Church but 'with' it in its perpetual task of conversion and renewal.

This chapter began with a reflection on the paradox of 'spiritual power'. With that thought we must also end. The Second Vatican Council recalled the whole Church to its origins. Ministry in the Church—including the papal ministry—exists not for its own sake but so that 'all who are of the people of God, and therefore enjoy a common Christian dignity, can work towards a common goal freely and yet in order' (*On the Church*, 18). Authority and community are like the two sides of a Gothic arch: they need each other. Community without authority soon disintegrates; and an authority which disregards the community it serves quickly becomes tyranny. The council defines the specific Petrine ministry in this way: 'the Chair of Peter presides over the whole assembly of charity and protects legitimate differences' (*ibid*, 13). That is the essential. Despite lamentable failures that no apologetic can justify, despite the assorted bric-à-brac of history that can mask fundamental truths, it is still possible to see a continuity in papal history. The Vatican embodies that continuity in the modern period: without the events in Nero's circus so long ago, it would be just another of the many hills of Rome.

---

6 Leaving the basilica, one is confronted with the whole panorama of Saint Peter's Square and its colonnades. An obelisk, seventy-seven feet high, stands in the middle. It was erected in four months in 1586 by 900 workers under the direction of the architect Domenico Fontana. The Via della Conciliazione, which runs in a straight line from the square to the Tiber and intersects an old quarter of the city, was built during the fascist era.

7 Saint Peter's Basilica is first and foremost a mausoleum, over which succeeding generations have built. Different levels, leading down from the present level of the papal altar, represent various epochs in the history of Christianity. Other tombs, dating from the time of Constantine the Great, have been found in the vicinity of Saint Peter's tomb.

8 The first basilica was built over the tomb of Saint Peter by the Emperor Constantine. Tradition has it that the Apostle was martyred in the nearby Circus of Nero. His tomb lies deep down beneath the papal altar. Attending a Papal Mass is the highlight of many a pilgrim's visit to Rome and the climax of the Mass, celebrated under the massive canopy, is the Pope's blessing. As the last words of the blessing are spoken, rapturous applause breaks out.

9–12 Every day, pilgrims and tourists pass through the immense portals of Saint Peter's. Cherubs on the holy-water font in the centre aisle give the visitor his first idea of the superhuman scale of the building. Popes and kings stand in niches, over doors and in the chapels. The bronze statue of Pope Pius XII is by Francesco Messina. One of the main attractions is the early Pietà by Michelangelo, in a side chapel.

13–14 The statue of the seated Saint Peter on the right-hand side of the nave, the work of the thirteenth-century sculptor, Arnolfo di Cambio, is an object of particular veneration for members of the faithful. Over the centuries, the hands of pilgrims seeking spiritual help have worn down the foot of the Apostle.

15–18 After the ceremonies in Saint Peter's, spiritual, diplomatic and political Rome get together. The Maronite Patriarch Khoraiche from the Lebanon pays his respects, while the Archbishop of Hanoi, Trin-nhu-Khuê (who has died since this photograph was taken) finds time to sign autographs. As Cardinal Bertoli chats with priests from the Eastern Church, Cardinal Pappalardo draws aside to have a conversation with a diplomat and his wife.

19–20 The Supreme Tribunal of the Apostolic Signature, the Sacred Roman Rota and the Apostolic Penententiaria make up the three courts of the Vatican. The Sacred Roman Rota, whose members meet the Pope officially for Mass and a reception every year, examine the civil and criminal cases which come to the attention of the Curia, and, above all, are responsible for the annulment of marriages.

21 The Sala Regia, originally intended for the reception of kings, was built in the luxurious and showy style of the late Renaissance by Antonio da Sangallo the Younger, during the pontificate of Paul III. Doors lead from it to the Sistine Chapel, the Scala Regia, the Capella Paolina and to the Sala Ducale.

22–23 Before the official opening of the Synod of Bishops in the Sistine Chapel by Pope Paul VI, bishops from dioceses around the world gather in the Sala Regia.

24–25 In the autumn of 1977, Paul VI officially opened the Synod of Bishop in the Sistine Chapel. After the ceremony, the papal Master of Ceremonies, Monsignor Virgilio Noè (right) and Monsignor Orazio Cocchetti escort the Pope back to his apartments.

26 Cardinals Pericle Felice (President of the Commission for the Revision of Canon Law) and Giovanni Benelli (Archbishop of Florence) lead the cardinals out of the Sistine Chapel after the opening Mass.

27 The Sistine Chapel, in which the cardinals gather in conclave to elect the Pope, is one of the greatest art-treasures of the world. In the reign of Sixtus V, masters of the early Renaissance from Umbria and Tuscany worked on the frescoes on the sides of the nave. Between 1508 and 1512, the young Michelangelo painted his gigantic cycle of ceiling frescoes showing the story of the Creation, scenes from the Old Testament and the powerful figures of prophets and sibyls—an immense undertaking in every sense, as he painted most of it lying on scaffolding. Decades later, he painted his 'Last Judgement' on the wall behind the altar.

28–33 The Synod of Bishops meets every three years. On the opening day, the Pope appears in the Audience Hall (which today bears his name) and prays with the bishops. Têtes à Têtes: Archbishop Marty of Paris and the Patriarch of Babylon, Paul II Cheiko; Cardinal Wright and Archbishop Sin of Manila; Archbishops Knox and Cordeiro (of Melbourne and Karachi respectively). Delegates are chosen for each session by their own Council of Bishops according to their expertise in the subjects being dealt with. Some faces, however, turn up for more than one session. Among these was that of the Archbishop of Cracow, Cardinal Wojtyla, who, in this way, came to the attention of the world episcopate. At the 1977 synod, Wojtyla walks across the room carrying his programme and some documents. Cardinals Vagnozzi, Willebrands, Luciani (later Pope) and Hume have already taken their places. The Secretary of State, Cardinal Villot, discusses a point with Cardinal Gantin while Archbishop Ribeiro of Lisbon and Archbishop Rubin listen in.

34–37 An Italian conversation: the urbane and much-travelled Cardinal Pignedoli, President of the Secretariat for Non-Christian Religions and Bishop Fallani, Secretary of the Commission for Sacred Art in Italy.

38–41 Pause for a cigarette: Cardinal Freeman, Archbishop of Sydney and Bishop John Mackey of Auckland.

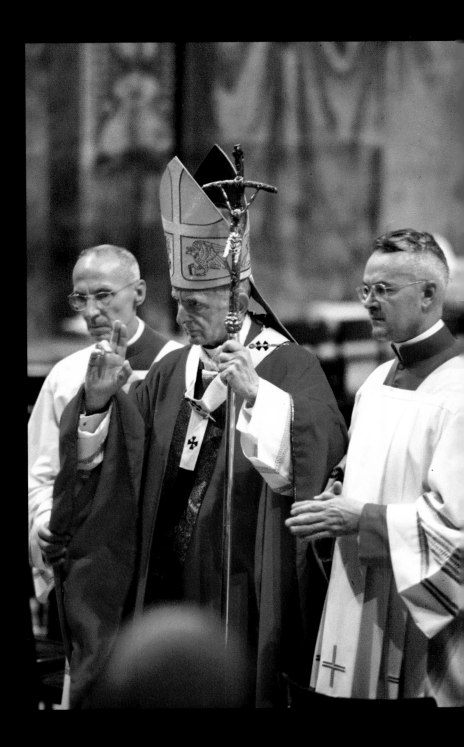

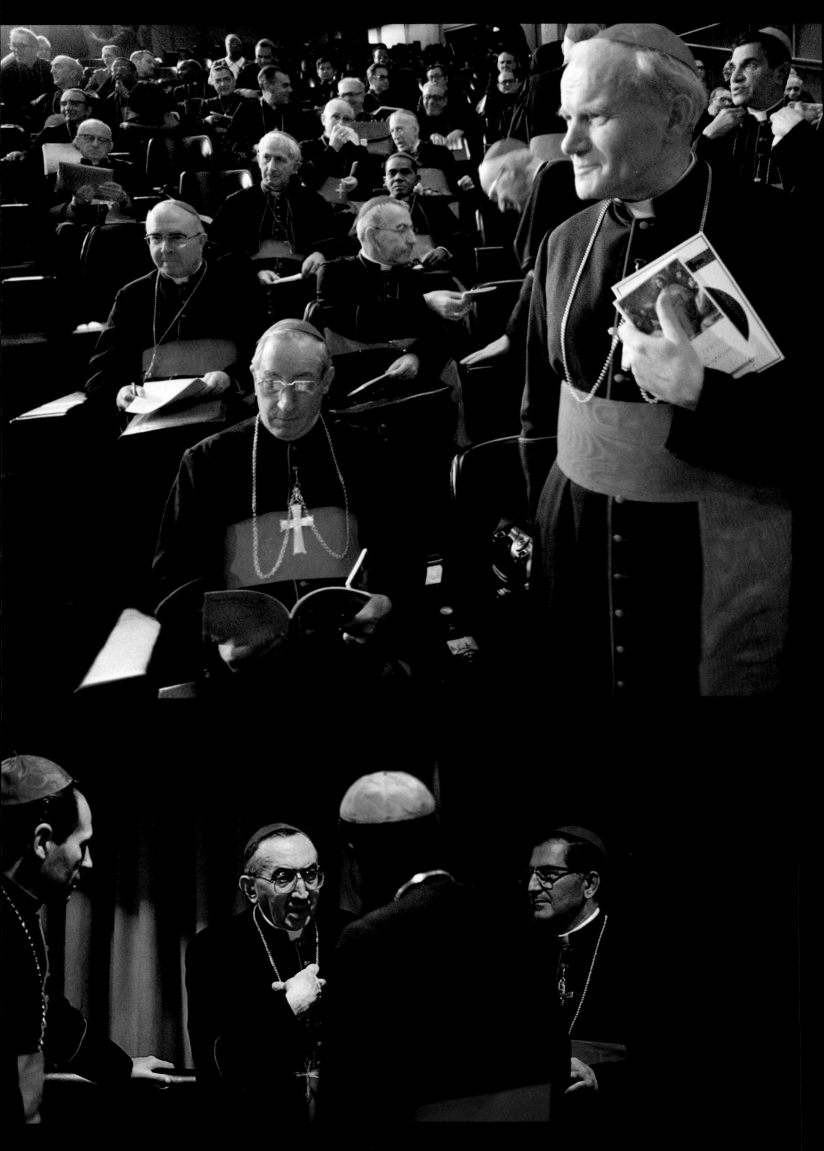

38–41

Sacerdotium and Imperium: Two Faces of the Vatican

Hanno Helbling

At the General Assembly of the United Nations during the last session of the Second Vatican Council, Pope Paul VI appeared before the delegates of the great and small powers represented in New York as the head of a very small state indeed. At the same time, some three thousand bishops from all over the world were meeting in Rome. They too represented millions of people within the whole *orbis terrarum*, or 'circle of the earth', and their gathering was derived from the oldest parliaments known in the West. Whereas the politicians assembled in New York formed an international body, the representatives of the Church gathered in Saint Peter's formed a supranational community older than the frontiers and alliances of the twentieth-century states.

The Pope knew, of course, that none of those listening to him in New York—not even the president of Italy at that time, Amintore Fanfani—were concerned about the walls and gardens over which the Pope ruled or about the staff who served him. For this reason, he did not remind them of his worldly kingdom, perhaps hoping to reply to Stalin's cynical question about the 'papal divisions'.

Paul VI preferred instead to draw attention to the Vatican state as a protected zone or a space of freedom that permitted the Church to preserve neutrality towards and distance from political events while devoting itself to its own tasks. In fact, the only aspects of worldly sovereignty that have been left to the Papacy are the independence and security guaranteed by the treaty with Italy. But these are, of course, also the most important aspects.

In the Middle Ages, it was believed that the Papal States, comprising much of Italy, had been given to Pope Sylvester I by the Emperor Constantine. Although untrue, the claim provided a convenient way of justifying the Church's secular power. It enabled the Church to assert that it did not possess this power in the world as of right, but only by the grace of the Emperor, just as the coronation of Charlemagne in Rome in 800 signified that the Emperor received his kingdom from the Pope. What *is* correct in the legend of the donation of Constantine, however, is that the Emperor, who had presided at the First Ecumenical Council of Nicaea in 325 and was baptised just before he died in 337, helped Christianity to become generally recognised, thus making it possible for the Church to establish a worldly rule within the Roman Empire.

'Alas, Constantine, how much trouble has been caused by your baptism, by your donation of the first kingdom to the Holy Father!' Dante exclaims in his *Divine Comedy*. On his passage through hell he is reminded of Constantine's gift by a Pope doing penance for his avarice. The rise of the Papacy to worldly power was, in Dante's opinion, so disastrous that he placed Constantine next to Adam in his vision of hell and went so far as to speak of a second fall. This is a harsh judgment, but its severity can be understood in the light of two factors, one religious and the other mainly political.

The religious reason for Dante's condemnation is to be found in Augustine's teaching about the two *civitates*, the earthly and the heavenly cities, states or kingdoms. The second of these moves in history through the first and reaches perfection at the end of time. Later on, the Reformers based their doctrine of the two kingdoms on a renewed understanding of the Augustinian teaching and developed it further, naturally enough giving it a strongly anti-papal emphasis. This opposition to the secularised Papacy had been present throughout the whole of the Middle Ages. Reforming groups of Christians and sects had always been active in their attempts to create a kingdom that was not of this world and a Church that owed allegiance only to the Spirit.

The second reason for Dante's attitude was political. He longed for Italy to become once again the great, united power that it had been in the Roman period. National and imperial ideas filled his mind and he regretted the division of the country. The Papal States formed a wide bar across Italy separating the north from the south. Those Italian cities outside the papal orbit that achieved independence soon began to fight among themselves, thereby attracting the attention of the more monolithic, but backward, powers north of the Alps. They were subjugated first by the Norman Emperor, then in turn by the Hohenstaufen, the Angevin kings, the house of Aragon and finally the Bourbons. Although despising these intruders, Italians tended to look to yet another foreign power for deliverance and a restoration of ancient unity: the Holy Roman Emperor. Dante placed his hope in the Emperor Henry VII just as Petrarch placed his in Charles IV. Both were from Luxemburg.

For centuries, the Popes thought of their own state as playing a very important part in international affairs. The Church needed a protected zone in order to be free of political influences in carrying out its spiritual mission: this was how the Church officially justified its position of power in the world. But the protected zone was and indeed had to be greater in the past than it is now, because it would have then been unwise to rely on respect for a merely symbolic sovereign power. It was, moreover, often very difficult to ensure the continued existence of the territory itself even if there were real means of power available. But the Pope's relationships with 'other' states, that is, those states which were purely political entities, were determined by the fact that he was regarded not as a sovereign lord in the usual sense of the word, but as the head of the Church of the Lord, whom he represented on earth as the successor of Peter.

For centuries, the Pope's relationships with the Emperor and the Empire were strained and difficult and he made use of political means to affirm his own position or, as it often seemed to his opponents, to reinforce it beyond the demands of reason. He formed alliances, went to war, concluded peace treaties and came between King and Emperor, father and son, city and state. He did all this in order to safeguard the space of his spiritual power or the 'sword of the Spirit' that, in his office as Pope, he had to use. Whenever the Pontiff was criticised for putting both the spiritual and the secular sword into one sheath, he would rightly return the criticism, just as the Emperor could easily claim a heavenly authority for himself that would have left no place for the Pope.

Sacerdotium and *Imperium*—priesthood and government—were opposed to each other, intermingled with each other, usurped each other and above all fought each other. This struggle went on for men who effectively had to serve two masters. Even if they were subjects of one of the Papal States and therefore dependent on only one authority, their freedom still remained precarious. The absolute power of the Pope weighed heavily on the country, and the governors serving under His Holiness kept two swords hanging over the heads of the citizens.

During the early period of the modern era, very few places gave so little encouragement to the spiritual life as the Papal States of central Italy. It was not until a division was made between *Sacerdotium* and *Imperium*, until the Papacy restricted itself to the exercise of a purely spiritual authority and the Italian state assumed the task of exercising secular power, that relationships within and around the Church were freed. The Church itself was the first to benefit from these improved relationships.

The Papacy regarded the reduction of its territory to the Vatican City as a mixed blessing. This reaction is not difficult to understand. On the one hand, neither the reunification of Italy as a nation, which took place in 1861 after a long struggle, nor the occupation of Rome in 1870 were seen as a service to the Church. What happened in Italy at this time was the fulfilment of the evolutionary process that had begun with the political dreams of Dante and Petrarch, dreams kept alive in the lamentations of poets and patriots and finally promoted, after the shattering experiences of the Napoleonic era, by politicians and conspirators. But the realisation of Italian nationalist aims had always or almost always met with opposition from the Popes.

Pius IX proved at first to be the exception to this general rule. At the beginning of his long pontificate, he was quite an enthusiastic patriot and had little sympathy for Bourbon rule in the south of Italy and Austrian domination in the north, despite their dynastic legality. He changed his mind, however, after the action of Garibaldi's volunteers against Austria in 1848. When the movement for the reunification of the Italian nation went so far as to insist on the incorporation of the Papal States into the new Italy, he became closed—and, perhaps more important, closed his Church—to the victorious tendencies of the period.

At the same time, the Popes continued to insist that their spiritual leadership or *Sacerdotium* should be given valid expression in the world and safeguarded in the presence of a state or *Imperium* that also derived its authority from higher principles. It was, however, now widely held that secular power was based not on God's grace granted to an anointed and consecrated ruler, but rather on a more or less liberal, national and decidedly secular ideology. In comparison with the Middle Ages, there was, then, both a release of tension and a sharpening of antagonism between the Church and the state. In the nineteenth century the struggle was no longer between each side in its attempt to justify its own sacred authority—papal power on the one hand and the power of the King or Emperor on the other. Instead, each side appealed to principles not recognised by the other.

When Rome was occupied by the Italian monarchy, which could, in the long run, be satisfied with no other capital city, Pius IX stayed as a prisoner in the Apostolic Palace and ceased to appear on the balcony of Saint Peter's to give his blessing to the people. During this period, several events occurred at about the same time, with both positive and negative results.

In the first place, the Pope's attitude brought Italian Catholicism into conflict with itself. Pius IX forbade Catholics to be politically active in the new Italy, where the Church had been deprived of many of its possessions and rights. In so doing he made almost all the Italian people choose either to reject the united Italy that had come about as a result of strenuous effort, patriotism and sacrifice or to disobey the Church. The offended Pontiff made it impossible for an Italian to be a good citizen and a good Catholic at the same time. This deprived Italian politics of the very forces that would have been able to represent the interests of the Church. The Italian clergy in particular took no part in political decision-making. Italian Catholicism remained politically unorganised and had no representative political party. As long as they did not become freemasons, however, politically committed individuals, many of them good Catholics, were able to participate in political activity. But the new state undoubtedly lost a source of potentially capable people. On the other hand it was from the very beginning free from ecclesiastical pressure.

Pius' protest against the ending of his secular authority may—precisely because this protest was both so radical and so sterile—have been only one aspect of his reaction. His successor, Leo XIII, knew that a purely moral authority could be a higher and more perfect form of authority. Would he, for example, have been able to publish the first social encyclical, *Rerum Novarum*, in 1891, if he had been politically and socially responsible for a part of Italy? The attention that should long before have been devoted to social questions in the Church as a whole (and which had in fact for some time been given in various national Churches) was now at last forthcoming. These social problems could not be considered by the Church as a whole until the Papacy had given up direct responsibility for the secular organisation of its own states. In its forced isolation from Italy and Rome, the Papacy was able to give greater emphasis to its universal dimension and to make itself—for Catholics at least—more credible. At the First Vatican Council in 1870, the primacy of Peter's successor and the infallibility of his dogmatic pronouncements were proclaimed, thus giving an absolute spiritual authority to the Papacy. This further weakened the Pope's links with the Italian state.

The Vatican, however, was in no hurry to become less Italian. The first real signs of decentralisation in the world Church appeared only after 1945, partly in connection with the process of decolonisation that was taking place at the time. Non-Italians were given leading positions in the College of Cardinals and the Curia and eventually, in 1978, a non-Italian cardinal was elected as head of the Church. Such developments are logical, for there has been every reason since 1870 for the Popes to make their spiritual rule international. Later the Church in Rome acquired a more decidedly local colour, just as the other local churches were anxious to become more autonomous. But the initial reluctance to decentralise was understandable. The Vatican wanted to keep its staff, all the members of which had been trained in the same way, but whose functions were now changing.

The loss of the Papal States led, for the first time since the age of Constantine, to a complete separation of the two 'swords'—the secular and the spiritual authorities. Here we have to try again to distinguish the two aspects of the same process.

If we consider the situation as it was in 1870 and ignore for the moment the developments that have taken place in the intervening years, we would probably believe that the Popes would have wished to divest themselves of all the attributes of secular power that still remained to them. Such a procedure as diplomatic relations with other states no longer seemed in accordance with the reality of the existing world situation. Conceivably, there would also have been a desire to get rid of such aspects of the Papacy as the Byzantine imperial ritual surrounding the person of the Pope, signs of subjection on the part of the Roman nobility and so on. The Church would continue to be present in the world in its teaching and its hierarchy. Those who professed to be Catholics would continue to adhere to the Church's directives in faith and morals, as would perhaps also Catholic bodies of various kinds.

In reality, however, things were very different. The papal nuncios remained in the capital cities of Europe; states that were represented at the Vatican by envoys continued to be thus represented and new diplomatic relations were added in the course of time. Paul VI became the first Pope to abandon the tiara and simplify the rites of the worldly ruler and John Paul I was the first to dispense with the coronation ceremony, perhaps more out of humility than consistency. In the years that followed the First Vatican Council, the forms of secular sovereignty persisted and were even supplemented by a policy of concordats. These agreements between states, in this case the papal state and various secular states, ensured that the Vatican had the right to establish churches and church institutions in certain individual countries. The Church thus made use of the secular arm—and, what is more, of an arm that went far beyond the scope of its own past authority—to realise its spiritual programme in such questions as marriage, education and Catholic associations of various kinds. Attempts were made, especially in Italy, to establish a state church to make up for the loss of the church state. An example of this can be found in the Concordat of 1929, whereby the Catholic prohibition of divorce was incorporated into Italian matrimonial law, thus making divorce illegal for all Italian citizens, including non-Catholics.

The possibility of a radical separation between the Church's secular authority and its spiritual power was, however, seen by the Popes as an opportunity to dispute the right of secular bodies to teach. In this context, it is important to note that the period when the Papal States disappeared and papal infallibility became dogma coincided with the time when Catholic doctrine was being most strenuously defended against those philosophies, ideologies and scientific principles that directly or indirectly presented a non-Christian or a post-Christian world-view. An example of the way in which attempts were made to protect Christian believers from influences believed to be hostile to faith was the addition, in brackets, to the quite correct summary of Darwin's evolutionary theory in the first Herder Lexicon: this does not apply to Catholics.

The Church's withdrawal from politics in Italy was in accordance with its neutrality towards political theories and movements throughout the world. The Church had a negative attitude towards politics as such. There are references in countless documents of the period to the 'poison' of liberalism or the 'plague' of communism as dangerous pseudo-doctrines of salvation. The political and social teaching of the Popes was conservative (rather as in Protestant Prussia), but it was also given a theological justification that was intended to raise it above the level of any party programme. Nonetheless, there had been, since the beginning of the nineteenth century, a political form of Catholicism in many countries which could only be expressed within the framework of secular convictions and movements. Even in Italy a Catholic party, the modern Christian Democrats, evolved. The Vatican has never, however, been able to accept without reservations that other positions can be equal to the Catholic position.

The concrete political involvement of Catholicism, as represented in the nineteenth century by the Papal States, has gradually diminished in the Church and will probably disappear altogether in the future. At the same time, the process that began in 1870 is also nearing its (positive) goal of a complete separation between secular and spiritual authority in the Church. The motivation underlying this development has not come either from an *Imperium*, a secular Church state, or from a *Sacerdotium*, the spiritual leadership of the Church, but from the world Church as a whole and its situation in a society consisting of states. The governments of these still continue to send representatives to the Holy See. These envoys spend the autumn of their careers in the Eternal City, while abroad, governments exchange greetings at their New Year receptions with the papal nuncio as the senior member of the local diplomatic corps. But the bishops in any country may well become restless if the nuncio enters into negotiations with their state or if he informs Rome about them or their possible successors, their faculties of theology or their clergy. The process of differentiation introduced by the council, continued by the Synods of Bishops and directed towards a meaningful social, cultural and political activity on the part of the Church has certainly not been furthered by the career diplomats of the Roman Curia. Good relationships with a government can only be maintained by the hierarchy of the country concerned. Bad relationships can easily occur if that government plays the nuncio off against the bishops. For these and similar reasons, a missionary bishop at the council called for the abolition of the nunciatures.

It was, moreover, not purely by chance that the demand was made by a bishop working in the Third World. The different relationship between the Church and social, cultural and political structures on the one hand and historical and religious structures on the other is particularly marked in the countries of the Third World. Since the time of Pius XI, the Popes have rightly attached a great deal of importance to the formation in these countries of a native clergy with the same ethnic origin as the laity. Reinforced by the Council, this policy has as its aim the creation of greater stability in local churches, the better to keep them from becoming foreign bodies in young, developing nations still striving to evolve their own identity. The objective is to eradicate everything that will remind the people of the connection between Christian faith and European oppression.

Other historical connections between the Church's authority and state authoritarianism also had to be broken. Paul VI questioned the ancient link between the Vatican and Spain, criticised the Latin American dictatorships and gave a minimum of support to the Italian clergy in their campaign against the government's proposals to revise the law on divorce. In failing to uphold one of the main features of the Concordat between the Vatican and an earlier government of Italy (a fascist one), the Pope showed his reluctance to insist upon the Church's political 'rights' in a secular but friendly state. He entered into agreements with communist governments whenever he believed that it was important to safeguard the external existence of the Church, perhaps at the expense of its inner development, but rightly avoided claiming privileges for the Church in countries where it was not threatened. In such situations, he preferred to let the Church, as a spiritual body, develop in the course of time a free relationship with secular powers based on partnership and open to criticism.

Whenever this policy was correctly understood by the Catholic clergy, it always benefited ecumenical relationships with other churches, especially since the abandonment of the Catholic claim to a monopoly of truth. In Rome, the Curia continued to exercise worldly power, but its effectiveness has continued to diminish over the years. The bishops meeting in synod in Rome, on the other hand, have concerned themselves with questions about the priesthood, the proclamation of the Christian message, moral theology and Christian education, all of which increasingly emphasises the spiritual aspect of the Church.

42 Accompanied by his secretary, Cardinal Trin-nhu-Khué, Archbishop of Hanoi, leaves the Secretariat of State.

43 Scene in front of Saint Peter's: as the French Ambassador makes a speedy departure, Archbishop Slipyj from Lvov in the Ukraine, who has spent 17 years of his life in Soviet jails and prison camps, is helped as he carefully negotiates some steps.

44 Saint Peter's Square, meeting place of all races: tourists from Nigeria stand in front of Bernini's colonades. Saint Peter's Square is the most visited square in the world.

45 Guests make their way along the corridor between the Bronze Portal and the Scala Regia. It was built by Bernini at the request of Pope Urban VIII.

46–48 En route to the Secretariat of State, the most important department of the Curia, a spectacular view of Saint Peter's Square and of Rome can be seen from the Loggia della Cosmografia, so-called because of the painted maps along the walls. These include maps of the Holy Land and Italy. Similar maps, showing the different provinces of Italy, are kept in the Sala del Mappamondo in the Museum across the way. On the other side of the Damasus Court is the Papal Palace. The Pope's private apartments are on the top floor.

49 The Logetta of Raphael is among the rooms occupied by the Secretariat of State. It is used as an ante-chamber and was decorated by Raphael and his pupils. Pope Leo X had it built for his secretary and former teacher, Bibbieno.

50–51 After the Secretary of State, the Deputy in the Secretariat of State, Monsignor Giuseppe Caprio, is the most important man in the hierarchy. This was even more so in the case of his predecessor, Monsignor Benelli, the present Archbishop of Florence. Visiting the Deputy are the General of the Jesuits, Father Pedro Arrupe, and the French Ambassador to the Holy See.

52 Seen here chatting with a guest, Monsignor Casaroli, titular Bishop of Carthage, a native of Northern Italy, is the Secretary of the Council for Public Affairs of the Church and 'de facto' foreign minister of the Vatican. His name has become known in both the East and the West through the 'Ostpolitik' of Pope Paul VI.

53–55 Cardinal Pignedoli, President of the Secretariat for Non-Christian Religions, has his residence in the Vatican. Here he receives guests from Japan, among them Shinto priests.

56 The Pope uses his private library for receiving heads of state, ministers and ambassadors of foreign governments, in private audience.

57–59 Smaller groups are received in the Room of the Evangelists in the Papal Apartments. The sculptures of SS. Peter and Paul on either side of the throne originally came from the old basilica.

60–62 Queen Margrethe of Denmark and her husband, Prince Henrik, in the papal private library. The Queen addresses the Pope. Later, she meets some of the people who work closest to him: Cardinal Villot, the Secretary of State, Monsignor Caprio and Monsignor Casaroli.

63–64 Every year, the Pope receives members of the diplomatic corps accredited to the Holy See, who come to pay their respects. Swiss Guards stand to attention in the Sala Clementina. In the Sala Consistoro, Paul VI talks to representatives of over a hundred diplomatic missions.

43

44▷

SYRIAE
PARS

INS PARS

MARE MEDITERRANEUM

VDASIVE CANANEA
ET PALESTINA
TERRA LACTE ET MELLE
FLVENS CHRISTVM NOBIS
FILIVM DEI
ET GENERIS HVMANI
REDEMPTOREM
DEDIT EX BETLEHEM
IVDA

ARA

BIAE

PARS

SCALA MILL.

MARE

ADRIATI

ITALIA PROVINCIARVM OMNIVM PVLCHERRIMA
SALVBERRIMA FRVCTVOSISSIMA
VIRIS DOCTRINIS ARMIS FRVGIBVS METALLIS
REBVS OMNIBVS AD COLENDAM VITAM
NECESSARIIS FLORENTISSIMA
OLIM REGINA GENTIVM
NVNC RELIGIONIS CHRISTIANAE PONTEQVE
SEDES AC VNICVM FERE VIRTVTIS
PERFVGIVM
LONGITVDINE AB AVGVSTA PRAETORIA
AD OPPIDVM REGIVM DECIES CENTENA VIGINTI
MILL PASSVVM LATTE VBI PLVRIMVM CC VBI
MINIMVM CXXXIV AMBITV AVARO AD ARSIAM
QVADRAGIES CENTENA MILLIA PASSVVM ET LVIII

DITERRANEO

MERIDIE

Papal Audiences

Victor J. Willi

In a very matter-of-fact world, few events are really able to make people happy. Papal audiences, however, can and do. For many Catholics and quite a few non-believers, an encounter with the Pope— any Pope—is a deeply personal experience. Many have summed it up, joyfully, as 'the most beautiful moment of my life'.

For a very long time, Wednesday has been the day of the general audience, when the Pope receives the people 'without rank and name' from the whole world. Indeed, countless thousands of visitors have been received in the basilica of Saint Peter itself and, since 1971, in the great auditorium that was designed for this purpose by the architect Pier Luigi Nervi. Twelve thousand people can be accommodated in this hall, but as the weeks go by, it becomes clearer that it is much too small to hold all those seeking an audience.

Everyone who enters the hall feels that he or she is one of those chosen from the many who seek admission. The apostolic prefect has the task of reconciling the supply with the demand for seats and standing room from one Wednesday to the next. Each of those fortunate enough to be admitted receives a ticket indicating the part of the auditorium or the row in which he or she will be sitting.

Every Pope fills the external framework of the audiences in the Vatican or at Castelgandolfo with his own personality, finds his own style and touches on certain needs that are felt by the Church and Christianity in general. A certain mystery emanated from Pope Pius XII, who could only be approached with deep respect as the 'aristocrat on the throne of Peter'. Many Christians instinctively went down on their knees before him. Kissing his ring was for them an immediate response to an inner urge, not simply a question of performing a ritual. This Pope satisfied the desire to express reverence, a longing felt by many people seeking security in a great community.

John XXIII proved to be quite different. It was not simply by chance that he ceased to use the royal 'we' when he spoke about himself. This break with tradition occurred, apparently for the first time, in an audience for the press at the beginning of Pope John's pontificate. It was on this occasion that he kept three hundred anxious journalists from all over the world waiting for forty minutes in the Sala Clementina. The relief of the pressmen was all the greater when the man who had recently been elected suddenly appeared before them and, despite his seventy-seven years and considerable corpulence, mounted the throne nimbly and began to speak in a lively voice. The erstwhile nuncio in Paris spoke in French, although even the French journalists present would have preferred an address in Italian. John XXIII noticed our embarrassment—and his own —and said, this time a little more clearly: *Moi, je parle le français comme ci comme ça!*

The new Pope won over the journalists with this reference to his own shortcomings. It was not long before he had gained the hearts of all men. The happy mood that made his audiences so memorable, and that brought all those who attended them together in unity, soon became known throughout the world. The roguish sense of humour of the man who came to be called *Il papa buono*—the good Pope—liberated human beings from their isolation.

It also changed very worldly soldiers into future angels. This happened in the courtyard of the Pope's summer residence at

65

Castelgandolfo. General Massu had lined up his parachute troops, the former masters of Algeria. They made a very war-like impression and John XXIII was obviously affected. He would undoubtedly have been a parachutist, he said, if such a unit had existed in the First World War. Then he added: 'If you can fall so bravely from heaven now, then make sure you go up there again.' People are bound to go on talking about John XXIII for a long time because he marked such an important break in the recent history of the Church and the Papacy.

John XXIII is said to have called Giovanni Montini 'Our Hamlet cardinal' when the latter was still the Archbishop of Milan. Awkward and full of doubts—even about himself and his mission—Paul VI confirmed this impression as Pope on many occasions, not least at his audiences.

He was extremely thoughtful and impressed those sensitive to his personality as being perhaps more critical of others and of himself than any of his predecessors. 'He was a Pope who gave us his suffering', one of his intimates wrote after his death. He believed that suffering was a precondition for being able to hold out against doubt and, with God's grace, to reach a higher certainty and an agreement with those who opposed the cause of good, especially communists and terrorists.

'Many people ask whether I am the Pope of the left wing or the Pope of the right wing. When will they understand that I am the Pope of all men?', Paul VI said to his secretary, Monsignor Macchi, long before Aldo Moro was seized and murdered. When the president of the Christian Democratic party, his close friend, was borne into Saint John Lateran ahead of all the leading politicians of his country on 13 May 1978 the funeral was seen on television screens throughout the world. At that time Paul VI spoke as the Pope of all humanity, as though all people were present with their everyday cares and needs.

After the Pope of suffering came John Paul I, the Pope of the smile—for thirty-three days. 'God just wanted to show him to us', Robert Kalt wrote on the day that he died. His death caused as much sadness as his brief pontificate had caused joy. For just over one month of our turbulent history, the cheerfulness of John Paul I had brought happiness to believers throughout the world. He had not sought the burden of the Papacy and as soon as this successor to Saint Peter had been elected he was overcome by a deep consciousness of the demands that his new office would make on him. 'May God forgive you', he told the cardinals in his first audience. The gentle John Paul may have had a premonition of his imminent end. Certainly no criticism was intended when he asked God to forgive them.

Four days later, in his first and last audience for the mass media, the new Pope pointed out in the same friendly and understanding way to the eight hundred journalists, radio and television people that they should keep to what was essential and not judge him by the size of his shoes or the colour of his socks. This was, of course, an allusion to his arrival in Venice as its patriarch in 1969. Then, many reporters had described his heavy country priest's shoes—'almost as long as gondolas'—and had lost sight of both the man wearing them and his important new mission as the city's archbishop.

This Pope, Albino Luciani, spoke to young and old throughout the world in images and lifelike parables and was understood by everybody. At the beginning of the Italian school year, he told an audience of children: 'When I was your age I had no idea that I would ever become Pope. Had I known, I would have learnt much more. Now it is too late. I am old now. But you are young and you can still learn a great deal.'

Five days later, John Paul I was dead and the world poorer. Humanity had lost a great hope. A voice had fallen silent, a voice that had been called from among men to make the Church a great auditorium for all humans, Christian and non-Christian alike, just as John XXIII, another Patriarch of Venice, had done.

After a short conclave, to everyone's surprise, the Vatican had a non-Italian Pope. There was, of course, immense interest in his first audience. In Nervi's splendid hall, people had waited a long time, sitting or standing for more than an hour. Many had remained at the entrance in order to be the first to witness the triumphant entry of Poland's Karol Wojtyla. Others were standing on the seats inside the great hall. In the open courtyard, children played hide-and-seek behind the columns and curtains; they even involved the grown-ups in the game. Representatives of every race, class and nation were there, exchanging friendly glances.

Each person present had his or her own personal history. A seventy-seven year old woman from Latina was sitting on the steps leading to the basement—the only free seat—and waiting for John Paul II. 'This Pope is like every other—our Pope', she said. 'It makes no difference, his coming from Poland. It is lucky that he can talk to us. And he can do that—not only in Italian.'

An old man from Taranto was visibly moved. He told me how for forty years he had come again and again with a group from his parish to general audiences with the last five Popes. 'It has always been a great event. The experience is always different, yet it is always the same', he told me.

The Swiss Guard did not find it easy to keep the enthusiastic throng at a safe distance and thus prevent their crushing the Pope when he entered the great hall. Luckily, the arrival of John Paul II was announced in five languages over the loud-speakers, followed by a commentary on the progress of the audience. Everyone therefore had a chance to partake of the proceedings on this unique occasion.

John Paul II arrived in an open car and received an ecstatic welcome in the antechamber. Whereas Pius XII appeared as a king and even John XXIII kept a certain distance from the people, the Polish Pope shook as many hands as possible, took children into his arms and let others hold him for a moment. Paul VI could not be so friendly and even John Paul I felt somewhat uncomfortable in the general audience. Or did all the Pontiffs express the same feeling in different ways?

The audience itself is always opened with the sign of the cross. However festive the mood, the suffering, death and resurrection of the Redeemer—the heart of Christian faith—is never forgotten in the presence of the Vicar of Christ. After greeting the cardinals, clergy and people, John Paul II received the different groups of pilgrims, each of which rose in turn to a great deal of hand clapping. Groups that had not been called, but were still chosen—groups like the Japanese who belonged to different faiths—were given the same applause as the Catholic groups. The Catholic Church can never be catholic enough.

The Poles enjoyed particular popularity, because they came from the Pope's own country. John Paul II addressed a few words to them and some Italians regretted that they could not understand Polish and that the new Pope was not Italian. However impressive his sermon in Italian on the virtue of overcoming weakness and however skilful its delivery, Karol Wojtyla remains the Pope 'who comes from a long way away' and he still cannot, owing to a lack of native fluency in Italian, express fully his spontaneous feelings of friendliness to those nearest to him.

John Paul II's third general audience on 15 November 1978 was dedicated to 'courage', the third of the cardinal virtues. 'Courage' was the word that a cardinal had whispered to his predecessor, John Paul I, when the latter was, to his great surprise, elected Pope by the Sacred College. Courage, declared the new Pontiff, is not simply something needed by the soldier on the battlefield, the mountaineer confronted by Everest or the astronaut surrounded by the vastness of the universe. (His choice of name alone showed whose work he wanted to complete.) Courage is above all something that the mother of an already large family needs when she says 'no' to the temptation to let a certain intervention take place.

The Pope's simple but very suggestive words evoked waves of applause in the auditorium, which was full to overflowing. People had come from far and wide to see John Paul II with their own eyes rather than simply look at his image on the television screen.

The Roman Church is Catholic, in other words, all-embracing, in that it is led by different Popes, each of whom appeals in his own way to different aspects of human nature, evokes different responses and represents different understandings of religious faith. There is no one obligatory papal style that must be expressed with a greater or lesser degree of success by all who hold this high office.

Some Popes please some people more than others: that is only human. According to the Catholic understanding of the Papacy, however, all Popes should please in some way that reflects the uniqueness of each. And somehow, they all achieve this aim. That is really what the old lady from Latina was saying.

65 *SCV 1: In his Mercedes, which bears the number plate SCV 1, Pope Paul VI is driven quickly from the Audience Hall to the Apostolic Palace. Kneeling Swiss Guards salute, their halberds in their right hands.*

66 *General audiences have taken on a new style since the inauguration of Pope John Paul II. Direct contact with the people has replaced ceremonious formality. Hundreds of hands reach out to the new Pope.*

67 *The arrival of the new Pope has increased the popularity of the Wednesday general audiences for tourists and pilgrims. Increased numbers have made it necessary to hold the audiences in two different locations—first in Saint Peter's and afterwards in the new Audience Hall, built by the Italian architect Nervi, which can hold up to 10,000 people. Everyone has to be in the hall hours before the Pope's arrival. Even these nuns, who work in the Vatican, have to use their identity cards to secure a better place for themselves and their party.*

68 *Pope Paul VI continued the tradition of having the Pope carried into the audiences on the* sedia gestatoria *by the* sediari *mainly so that he could be seen by everyone. Pope John Paul I wanted to do away with the chair of state, but was persuaded to continue using it. His successor, however, would not be persuaded, and walks through the Audience Hall on foot.*

69–70 *Scenes of unbounded rejoicing and excitement as Pope John Paul II walks through the crowd, shaking outstretched hands.*

71–72 *Every Sunday at midday, a colourful crowd turns up in Saint Peter's Square for a rendezvous with the Pope, high up in the window of his study. He addresses a few words to them, referring to things of relevance to the city and the world. This leads up to the recitation of the Angelus, the traditional prayer of the people, which is said at midday and in the evening. Pope John Paul I, who took over the custom from Pope Paul VI, had only a few opportunities to carry out this part of his role as parish priest to his city and to the rest of the world.*

73 *View over the papal throne into the Sala Clementina, one of the many magnificent rooms in the Apostolic Palace. It is used for the reception of larger groups.*

Daily Life in the Vatican

Peter Nichols

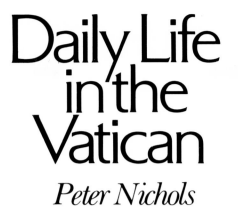

Holy men in the desert used to show their zeal and display their faith by living for years at a time on the top of a column, or pedestal. The Pope rules over a tiny state which has been described as a tiny pedestal supporting the Holy See, the spiritual centre of Catholicism throughout the world. Daily life in Vatican City has nothing much of the rigours of living on a desert hermit's pedestal, except for a few unusual disciplinary measures which its inhabitants must observe, such as the closing of the gates at night, a certain degree of moral behaviour required of them (drunkenness, for instance, is frowned on, as is abuse of tax-free privileges) and the very low speed-limits imposed on motor traffic. The concept, however, is the same. The state of Vatican City is the material basis for the exercise of a vast spiritual power, and this curiously uneven relationship, yet logical combination, is constantly reflected in the life of its citizens and residents.

The state certainly is tiny, a bare 108.5 acres. The principality of Monaco is three and a half times bigger, Liechtenstein three hundred times larger and San Marino, the world's smallest republic, is 138 times the size of this totally landlocked and walled enclave within the city of Rome. Its maximum length is 1,132 yards and at its widest it is 812 yards across. Inhabitants taking a walk around the whole state will note that its internal balance is three-fold: a third is courtyards and squares, some of them very beautiful and others featureless; a third is covered by buildings, including the Apostolic Palace at one extreme and a laundry collection point at another; a third consists of gardens. A small (and enclosed) section of the gardens is given over to vegetables while the rest provides some of the most sumptuous views in the world in an exquisite combination of nature and human creation.

Life goes on against a background which must strike the inhabitant at four levels at least. In terms of size and population it is a village, not a city or a state, yet its present boundaries closely follow the walls built by a succession of four Popes from 1540 to 1640. The historically-minded inhabitant will know that the Catholic Church has been ruled from the Vatican only since 1377 when Gregory XI came back from Avignon: earlier Popes had lived in the Lateran from the time it was given to them by the Emperor Constantine. But the site itself had the far more ancient distinction of being the place traditionally said to have been the ground where Saint Peter was martyred and buried. The Vatican state can also be looked on as the last vestige of the papal territories which at the height of the Papacy's temporal power dominated Central Italy and embraced the whole city of Rome. Finally, a citizen sensitive to the character of the place might feel it to be an artificial creation, established by treaty between the Papacy and Italy as part of a series of agreements by which peace was made in 1929. The long quarrel had begun in 1870 when the Italians took over the last of the Pope's dominions—Rome itself—in the process of uniting their country. Certainly a touch of this artificiality remains. The Swiss Guard with their striped uniforms and halberds, the excellently preserved courtyards, the stately quiet of the gardens, are all apt to give a theatrical impression, suggesting a setting where rehearsals are about to begin rather than the scene of a drama already begun. To a person familiar with the Vatican, the tiny state has the most unexpected air of all: despite the solemn grace of the palace, the awareness that the buildings contain some of the greatest masterpieces devised by the human mind, the massive structure of the basilica, it has a touch of the provisional. This is not so much the case in Saint Peter's itself, or the papal palace, except to the extent that the personality of each Pontiff changes the atmosphere as well as the decorations. But outside, in the squares and administrative buildings, the feeling is perceptible.

Daily life in the Vatican is a constant reminder of each of these elements. Certainly it is all that the Pope now possesses as a sovereign although he once ruled over territories that included the present regions of Umbria, Lazio, the Marches and Romagna. But he remains a supreme autocrat. The reduction of his once widespread possessions to this minute corner has in no way diminished the absolute nature of his rule. The Fundamental Law of Vatican City which came into effect on 7 June 1929 states without equivocation in its first article: 'The Supreme Pontiff, sovereign of the State of Vatican City, has the fullness of legislative, executive and judicial powers.' There must be few other sovereigns in the western world accorded such unquestioned personal authority. But smallness makes for intimacy. 'We often see the Pope', one lady, who is a citizen, says, 'when we are sitting on our balcony.' The Vatican, again unexpectedly, retains this touch of informality despite the presence of the palaces and the works of art and the survival of autocratic rule. The feeling is not only due to the intimacy imposed by so small an area, though this helps.

The number of people living in Vatican City is small, and purposely kept to the essential minimum. The general tendency is for it to drop. In 1932 the population was little more than a thousand: in 1936 it was 946 of whom 736 had citizenship and the remainder were residents; at a count made on 21 September 1978, the total number of citizens was 392 and residents without citizenship amounted to 339, making a total of 731 inhabitants.

There is a clear distinction made between residents and citizens. The largest single group of citizens entitled to carry the little red Vatican passport is made up of the Pope's diplomatic corps which numbers 179. They all have full citizenship while working in this capacity. Nobody can be born a Vatican citizen. The status comes as a consequence of particular functions. The second-largest group of citizens is made up of the eighty members of the Swiss Guard, the Pope's last remaining armed forces. And then come the thirty-six cardinals resident in Rome: some of the cardinals working in the Curia do not live inside the Vatican City but are citizens all the same. The list includes thirty-three priests and members of religious orders who are citizens, four nuns, thirty laymen and the same number of women. The residents without citizenship in autumn 1978 consisted of 131 priests and members of religious orders, 126 nuns, seventeen laymen and sixty-five women. Everyday life in the Vatican is dominated by men, who number 506 as compared with 225 women, quite different from the situation on the other side of the walls in Italy where women outnumber men.

Residents and citizens alike know that they are living in this particular area, under a totally unique set of regulations and circumstances, for two reasons. The first is a combination of history and religious faith. In ancient times, the area was regarded as neither desirable nor salubrious. When the Romans spoke of the *Vaticanum*, they referred to a much larger zone than what is now known as Vatican City and usually did so in terms of considerable dislike. For them the Vatican began at Monte Mario, or even beyond it, and came down as far as the Janiculum hill to the south while being bordered to the east by the Tiber. It included hills and a plain along the river with small villages dating from Etruscan times where potters and farmers lived. This lowlying land, frequently flooded by the Tiber, was marshy and generally regarded as unhealthy. Tacitus says that the army of Vitellius, Vespasian's enemy, was plague-stricken because it had camped 'in the infamous area of the Vatican', and according to Martial the vines produced a wine that tasted of vinegar. When the Audience Hall was built for Paul VI in 1971 the architect, Nervi, encountered difficulties in finding firm enough ground to support his huge structure.

Under the Empire, the Vatican neighbourhood began to change. Caligula's mother, Agrippina, built a luxurious country house there, and so did other patricians. Caligula himself built his famous circus, in the centre of which he placed the obelisk brought from Egypt in a specially constructed galley. Now a familiar landmark, it stands in the centre of

Saint Peter's Square. Nero added to the circus and used it as one of the places in which Christians were martyred. According to tradition, Saint Peter was one of them and, after his crucifixion upside down, was buried there. And so the spirit of place, the atmosphere enveloping the area, underwent its strange metamorphosis from a large zone considered extremely disagreeable to a retreat for patricians and then as the most famous centre of Christendom. The term Vatican came to mean something quite different: a more concentrated area, holy to the point of requiring walls around it to defend it from barbarians and later invaders. The first walls went up in 852, six years after a marauding party of Saracens had sacked Saint Peter's. Later Popes extended the area within the protecting system of walls until the present pattern was reached in the seventeenth century. The enclosure is broken by Saint Peter's Square itself. There are now three entrances, but since all of them are locked at night, the resident must still feel, despite the modern additions within the wall, that the city has something of the character of a sacred citadel. The little state in which they live is one of the very few examples of a place which has not been shaped by geography, by convenience or even by choice but by this mixture of history and faith.

The second reason why the residents are there and live as they do is also historical but of much more recent date. The Vatican City state came into existence in its present form as a result of the treaty with Italy ratified on 7 June 1929, which still has its effect on disciplining life within the precincts. By that treaty, the Popes retained sovereignty over the ancient nucleus of the Christian presence in Rome. The fact that the Vatican is a papal possession, recognised internationally as a state, is important. Some territorial basis was deemed necessary in order to enable the Papacy to conduct its mission, and this conviction was well expressed by Pope Pius IX in 1871, just a year after he had lost all his territories and retreated into the Vatican palace. He told the French Ambassador: 'All that I want is a small corner of earth where I am master. This is not to say that I would refuse my states if they were offered to me, but so long as I do not have this little corner of earth, I shall not be able to exercise my spiritual functions in their fullness.' This is the fundamental explanation for the existence of this anomalous little state.

Even if anomalous, the Vatican has all the attributes of statehood. It has its own flag which consists of two fields divided vertically, the one next to the staff yellow and the other white, bearing the crossed keys and the tiara. It has its own posts and telegraphs, its own law courts, a railway station connected by branch line to the Italian system, a chemist's shop managed by members of a religious order (the Fatebenefratelli), a newspaper, a radio station, a shop selling groceries and another dealing mainly in clothes and household requirements. It mints coins and prints highly-prized postage stamps. It is entitled to a fleet flying its own flag, though so far it has made no use of this right.

Citizens and residents can find all that they need to support life within the walls. And on favourable terms. There are no taxes and so goods in the two shops are cheaper than in Italy. Income tax and value added tax do not exist. There is a petrol pump, and those entitled to use it pay only three-fifths of the high Italian price (300 instead of 500 lire a litre). Clothing in the shop under what is known as the governor's offices (though there is no governor) is strikingly well chosen. Cashmere, British suit-lengths, clothes drawn mainly from the best British and Italian suppliers are remarkably cheap. Blankets, sheets, radios, watches: it is a well-stocked shop indeed. The four types of commerce—foodstuffs, clothing, petrol and tobacco—are all that the rules permit. A citizen or resident of the Vatican cannot decide to open a shop or business. A market economy does not exist there. But demand remains strong for what is already available. The foodshop known as the 'Annona', from the Latin word meaning a year's crops and produce, is frequently packed. Only authorised shoppers may use it and those with permits number 7,000. One housewife who is a citizen remarked that she seldom goes there because of the crowds. She usually manages to persuade her husband to go immediately it opens, to buy what they need and to make purchases for friends. A good deal of co-operation exists among residents, so that one person can buy for more than one family. A few of the more idealistic inhabitants say that these privileged places for shopping ought not to be allowed because the sight of bulging shopping bags and impatient queues at the cashier's desk strikes too materialistic a note. Others argue that salaries are unusually low in the Vatican and it is only reasonable that the little city's statehood should be exploited to provide a fair and just barrier against the effects of inflation.

Attempts are made to keep shopping within proper bounds so that these privileges are not blatantly abused. A form of rationing is applied to petrol, tobacco and alcohol. Occasionally there are official protests from the Italian side against alleged abuses but the Vatican authorities maintain that in most cases the allegations are exaggerated. And sanctions are applied when abuse is uncovered. A museum custodian, for instance, lost his shopping rights after it was discovered that he was supplying a local restaurant with cheap butter in return for supper each Saturday night for himself and family.

The real point about salaries is less that they are low than that there is little difference between the various grades of pay by comparison with other societies. The maximum monthly salary is about 700,000 lire. This is the pay of a civil servant at the top of the Vatican's administrative hierarchy, or of a cardinal. Comparatively few officials, much lower down the scale, earn less than 300,000 to 350,000 lire a month. Laymen with families receive family allowances of 17,000 lire a month for each child. Cost-of-living rises are given and severance pay on the generous Italian pattern is now general practice. This allows for payment on retirement of a month's salary for every year worked at the Vatican. There is also a regular pension scheme. A retiring employee can choose between a full pension, which is the equivalent of his final salary, or severance payment and 80 per cent of his final salary. There is now also a system by which money can be borrowed as an advance of salary.

Inhabitants of the Vatican noticed sweeping changes in the field of employment, of labour relations, working conditions, pay and pensions as a result of the late Pope Paul VI's conviction that change was essential. He was a Pontiff concerned about social questions and his reign coincided with new demands by labour in Italy, demands which could hardly have left the Vatican untouched. He issued a long series of documents which transformed the paternalistic and somewhat haphazard way in which administration at the Vatican had been conducted. In the past, much depended on personal relationships and family considerations. Something of this remains but, generally, applicants for posts take part in competitive examinations, or are chosen for some specific skills—specialist restorers, for instance, or workers in mosaic. The principal decree laying down regulations governing employment was issued in July 1969 and is a full document of sixty-three pages and 132 articles, designed to establish employment in the Vatican firmly on the basis of law and no longer on whim or favouritism. Insistence on legality was also intended to put aside suspicions that informality might cloak dishonesty. The success of this aim is difficult to measure. A priest who is a resident and a citizen stated that while the level of public morality was not as low in the Vatican as in Italy, not everything was perfect.

Employment and administration are both strongly marked by one of the totally unique aspects of life at the Vatican, and one which is felt at all levels. All employment at the Vatican, like property, is public, not private. All work is in the hands of the state administration and controlled by it. There are no unions. The state has a monopoly in the labour field just as it has in housing. There is a story of a Syrian diplomat who was trying to explain to a prelate at the Vatican the virtues, as his government saw them, of state ownership of everything. He was quietly reminded that nowhere did such a system function so fully as within the walls of the Vatican. Everything, from the number of cigarettes which can be bought without duty (forty packets a month) to the running of the museums or the embarking on public works, depends directly on the state. Apart from the fascination of so complete a system, it has one unfortunate aspect. Employees working in the Vatican who are neither residents nor citizens— they number about 2,500—find that their salaries are worked out on the basis of the advantages which residents enjoy in such important areas as housing. But they must live in Italy, where the economy is not shaped to fit the needs of the inhabitants in the way it is in the Vatican. They live between two worlds, rents being one of their worst problems.

The affairs of this little state may depend directly on the Pope but he can hardly be expected to deal with administrative details which are therefore made over to a committee of cardinals, known as the Pontifical Commission for the Vatican City state. Its seven members are appointed for five years, which is something of a magic figure in the modern Vatican's world. Paul VI introduced the idea that holders of important offices in the Catholic Church's government should have their tenure brought up for renewal every five years and the principle is applied as well to the administration of the state. The aim is to allow the fullest flexibility to a Pope who wishes to renew the higher echelons of his bureaucracy.

This Pontifical Commission is presided over by the Cardinal-Secretary of State. He attends its meetings but he also has a cardinal pro-President who follows the work of the administration on a daily basis. The full commission meets about once a month. Apart from the cardinal pro-President, the principal executive is a layman with the title of 'special delegate', the present holder being the Marchese Giulio Sacchetti, a member of a leading family of the hereditary papal nobility. This system also derives from Paul VI who introduced it in July 1969. It includes another body, known as the 'Consulta'. The eminent laymen of this consultative committee do not belong to the Vatican's administration but can be called on to give advice.

The offices of the administration are immediately behind the apse of Saint Peter's. Inhabitants who go there for bureaucratic reasons or to visit the shop under the building can, when leaving, at least feel the satisfaction of facing one of the most beautiful views in the world—the basilica lightened by the cypresses and pines which mark its huge walls.

The administrative building was not designed as such. Originally it was intended for two purposes: as the minor seminary for the Rome diocese and also as the state apartments for visiting dignitaries. The room in which the Pontifical Commission holds its meetings on the first floor was designed as the throne room for the use of royal guests. The office of the Secretary-General of the administration, Dr Vittorio Trocchi, was planned to be the bedroom of the Pope's guests and retains the ornamental weight and substance of formal apartments of the time.

Paul VI in his reforming zeal did away with one of the most colourful aspects of Vatican life by abolishing all the armed forces with the exception of the Swiss Guard. The decision came in the form of a letter from the Pope to Cardinal Villot, his Secretary of State, and decreed the end of the Noble Guard, the Palatine Guard and the Pontifical Gendarmes, all of whom had lent colour to the little city with their archaic uniforms. 'In your quality', the Pope wrote to Cardinal Villot on 14 September 1970, 'of our first collaborator, you cannot but be aware of our will to see that everyone who surrounds the Successor of Peter shows clearly the religious character of his mission, always most sincerely inspired to follow a line of genuine evangelical simplicity.' From this slightly forbidding beginning, the letter goes on to announce the decision to dissolve the armed forces, given that they no longer fitted the needs for which they had been instituted. His decision was in keeping with his re-decoration of the Apostolic Palace which was traditionally hung with burgundy coloured damask and gold: he made the dominant colours beige and grey.

Daily life, however, does not much turn on the life of the palace. Certainly each Pope creates a different atmosphere which passes beyond the palace to the state itself. Pius XII was so remote as to be practically non-existent as a person to the inhabitants. John XXIII was likely to appear anywhere on his explorations of his state which he hardly knew before his election. Paul VI was again personally remote and spent most of his leisure time on his roof-terrace rather than in the gardens. But he made a deeply-felt impression in the field of legislation. John Paul I had even more to discover than did John XXIII and started to do so with a ready smile. His successor, John Paul II, already knew the Vatican better on his election and has brought to it a personal impact stronger than that of any Pope within living memory, as befits the first non-Italian to rule for more than four hundred years.

But ordinary citizens have more to do with the administration of everyday matters than with the sovereign in person. The structure of the administration indicates the order of importance attached to the various departments and the method of dividing the work of conducting the state's internal affairs.

The department most closely in contact with daily life in the Vatican is that known as the General Secretariat. It includes, apart from general affairs, the philatelic and numismatic offices, the office for legal affairs, the personnel office, the accountancy office, posts and telegraphs, goods and the city's tribunal of first instance in matters concerning administration and personnel. This is one of the Vatican's three courts. The others are the tribunal dealing with appeals and the courts of cassation. Most of the legal business which comes before the city's courts is concerned with employment and labour relations. At these hearings, the Secretary-General himself acts as the Vatican's state attorney.

The second department handles the business of monuments, museums and galleries, including the Vatican's famous laboratory for repairs and restoration. The most dramatic work of the restorers in recent times was the repairs done to the *Pietà* of Michelangelo after it had been seriously damaged by a mentally unbalanced visitor to Saint Peter's. The third department deals with general services, with building, the state's fleet of cars (all bearing the Vatican's SCV on the number plate), the telephone system and exchange (now worked by an efficient group of nuns) and, finally, with the famous store rooms known as the 'Floreria'. These contain furniture, pictures, statues, beds, carpets, ornaments, bookcases, busts, candlesticks, peacock feathers, stuffed animals, all of them possessions of former Popes or the Vatican but put away because they no longer find favour with the reigning Pontiff. The men who work there include carpenters, weavers, painters and cabinet makers. An example of what can be found there is the brass bed in which Pius X slept. It had originally been used by Pius VII. When Pius X was elected, they polished the old bed and put it into the papal apartment, commenting that it was a beautiful bed. The Pope agreed, adding: 'But I shall die in it.' So he did, whereupon it went back to the stores.

The fourth department concerns Vatican Radio, and includes a technical service, and offices dealing with programmes and preparing news bulletins. Its main offices are above the basilica in a building erected by Gregory XIII in 1579. Originally it housed an anemoscope and the famous meridian which tradition says convinced Gregory of the need to reform the calendar. From 1797 it became the Vatican's observatory and after this was moved to the Pope's summer residence at Castelgandolfo, the scientific traditions of the building were maintained by the placing there of a transmitter designed by Guglielmo Marconi. The ornate microphone with which a Pope's words were first broadcast is still in the office of Father Roberto Tucci, the Radio's director. The observatory, known as the Specola, is administered, like the radio, by a department of its own. There are separate departments dealing with economic and health services, archaeological research and, finally, one for the administration of the pontifical villas at Castelgandolfo.

Castelgandolfo forms part of the life of the papal household rather than of everyday life in the Vatican itself. From July to September the Pontiff moves to this town in the Alban Hills south of Rome with its spectacular view on to Lake Albano. On two recent occasions, however, the summer residence became, very dramatically and sadly, the centre of the Vatican's life. Pius XII died there in 1958 and Paul VI on 6 August 1978, the only two Popes to do so. On both occasions the streets of the little town were full of familiar faces from the state itself, as well as with the faces of the faithful and the curious who would have been thronging Saint Peter's Square had the Pope died within the frontiers of his walled sovereign state.

Security is essential in the Vatican. There is nowhere else on earth where violence could do so much damage in so short a time and in so small a physical place, quite apart from the effect that a physical attack on the Pope himself would have on international opinion. The destruction of the Sistine Chapel, or the contents of the Library or the Archive, even acts of resolute vandalism where works of art or religious sites are not involved, such as damage to the gardens or the fountains, would generate shocks out of all proportion to the actual damage done. The Vatican is a terrorist's paradise in the full distorted sense of the term. And so security too is part of the atmosphere of everyday life in the state. It still feels wrong but its necessity cannot be denied. Furthermore the Vatican has taken its own steps to deal with the threat of personal violence as well as to meet the danger of a nuclear holocaust. All states are subject to these threats, the Vatican among them.

Crime and violence within the city are so far practically unknown. The city boasts no places that might encourage rowdiness or misbehaviour in its citizens: no bars to brighten the evenings, no restaurants, still less any night clubs. There is not a neon-lit advertisement to be seen. It is in fact devoid of any form of what is usually regarded as entertainment. The closing of the gates at night means that long evenings amidst the plentiful pleasures of Rome are difficult unless they go on long enough to finish around the opening of the gates in the early morning. A citizen resident in the Vatican cannot expect to have a full social life in the normal sense of the term. As might be expected, such violence as occurs comes from outside. Occasionally people, mostly young people, are caught trying to scale the walls, presumably more for the excitement of doing so than for any other specific object. Once in the last two decades a bomb was exploded at one of the gates by a somewhat highly strung young actor, but it did no serious damage. These are pale, very pale, echoes of the old danger from the barbarians: echoes, or possibly, in some cases, signs of a more threatening world which is growing up around the Vatican.

The present security system was established by decree of Paul VI in February 1971 in which he laid down the regulations for the city's Central Office of Vigilance. This body placed security on a new footing, essential after the dissolution of the papal gendarmerie, when all the Pope's armed forces except the Swiss Guard were abolished. Some of the former gendarmes were in fact taken into the new service.

To the ordinary public, these security guards seem omnipresent. The Swiss Guard look splendid at the main entrances to the city and they normally ask visitors and citizens, if they do not know them well by sight, where they are going. But beyond the Swiss Guard there is another office, manned by these security guards, where the real checking is done. It is possible to pass without much trouble if the person one is going to meet has informed the guards of the appointment and arranged for a permit to be ready. Once past the gate, the visitor will encounter other security guards at main corners within the city or patrolling the gardens. They maintain a fairly continuous checking service and those inside frequently telephone to the gatehouse in order to confirm that an unfamiliar car registration belongs to a person who has entered the state legitimately.

The regulations governing the work of these security guards typify the Vatican, a tiny territory which is nevertheless of great importance as the seat of the Pontiffs. The first of their duties is to maintain 'awareness of the value of the promise of fidelity to the Supreme Pontiff, which implies the strict observance of the orders imparted by superiors, and the responsible and diligent execution of their tasks and special duties assigned to them. . . . The tasks of each are not limited materially only to the execution of what they have been ordered to do, but include all that alert and unceasing activity which, by discovering, anticipating and restraining every action contrary to the laws and rules, makes up the singular character of those who are concerned with vigilance and the defence of order, the safety of persons and the safeguarding of material goods.'

Paul VI was rumoured to be a target for a group of West German terrorists. His immediate successor, the short-lived John Paul I, was anxious to move freely outside the Vatican, pursuing what he felt to be his pastoral obligations to the Rome diocese. He had to be reminded of the seriousness of the security issue now that he had ceased merely to be one of a number of cardinals. Pope John Paul II is no doubt more aware of the security question, coming from Eastern Europe. He is, however, inclined to be unpredictable and is ready to break the bonds of protocol, thereby straining the security measures taken for his protection. His reign had hardly begun, moreover, when he started his Sunday journeys outside the Vatican, sometimes using a helicopter.

Another element has increased the feeling of the need for security within the Vatican. Since the closing years of Paul VI, the Papacy has become increasingly popular in the sense that a growing number of people want to see the Pope in person, while his own little state grows no larger and cannot do so unless the treaty with Italy were to be re-negotiated, which is almost unthinkable. This popularity has grown still more striking with John Paul II's great ability to handle crowds and his attractiveness as a personality. It is almost impossible totally to assure a Pope's life and person against attack.

When Paul VI addressed the first general audience to be held in Nervi's Audience Hall on 30 June 1971, he said, 'We can make our own, and apply to the service for which this hall was designed, the words that Saint Paul wrote to the Romans: "for I long to see you, that I may impart to you some spiritual gift to strengthen you, that is, that we may be mutually encouraged by each other's faith, both yours and mine." '

The sentiments are fine. They go some way towards refuting the criticisms of the hall as being out of keeping with the view that the Papacy play a less prominent role within the Church and the ordinary bishops a more prominent one. The phenomenon they describe goes far beyond the concept of security. It embraces the place of the Papacy in its relationships both within the Catholic Church itself and outside it. The 'tiny pedestal' indeed has more people coming to see it. There would be an increasing number of residents, too, given the growing functions of the Papacy and its offices, were it not papal policy to keep this somewhat mixed privilege to a minimum.

The Registry whose task it is to compile and conserve the registration of births, marriages and deaths as well as to record citizenship and residence, when granted, is unlikely to have its capacities unduly tested in the forseeable future, whatever changes may take place in other realms of the Catholic Church.

But the city will never become static. It is always and essentially the residence of the Popes who at the same time are, formally speaking, its absolute masters. But as Popes vary in character, personal habit and tastes, this variation affects the sovereign's immediate environment, which is the Vatican City.

74 On its northern side, the view of the Vatican City is dominated by the powerful buildings of the Vatican Museums, with their corridors and courtyards. The Giancolo Hill, dotted with woodlands and colleges, rises above the circle formed by Bernini's colonnades.

75 Nuns return to the Porta Sant'Anna, the busiest gate into the Vatican City. It is patrolled by the Swiss Guard and the Vigilanza, the Vatican police force. The round building in front of the Papal Palace houses the Vatican Bank, the 'Instituto per le Opere di Religione' which is under the direction of the American Monsignor Marcinkus.

76 For the most part, the present-day boundaries of the Vatican City coincide with the walls built by Pope Leo IV in the ninth century, as a defence against Saracen raids. Later, they were strengthened and widened in the Renaissance and Baroque eras, under Paul III and Urban VIII. They are an extension of the original Aurelian Walls which enclosed the ancient city of Rome on the other side of the Tiber.

77 With their left hands holding the flag and their right hands raised in oath, newly-appointed members of the Swiss Guard swear to serve the reigning Pope and his rightful successor in true and upright manner, and, if necessary, risk life and limb in defending them. Any male Catholic citizen of Switzerland, who has successfully completed his training at the recruiting school, and who is single, at least 5 feet $8\frac{1}{2}$ inches tall and between the ages of nineteen and twenty-five, can present himself for membership of the papal bodyguard.

78–80 Wearing their red, yellow and blue gala uniforms, the Swiss Guard commemorate their day of honour on 6 May with the swearing-in ceremony. On 6 May 1527, 147 of their members were killed in Saint Peter's Square and in the basilica during the Sacco di Roma, *thus enabling the Pope, Clement VII, to escape to the Castel Sant'Angelo under the protection of forty-two members of the Guard. Archbishop Benelli, former Deputy in the Secretariat of State, presents an award to a member of the Guard. Between them is the Commandant, Colonel Franz Pfyffer.*

81–82 Day and night, the Swiss Guard patrols the three main entrances to the Vatican (Porta Sant'Anna, the Bronze Door and the Arco delle Campane). They also guard the entrances to the Papal Palace and provide a guard of honour at Church ceremonies, audiences and receptions.

83–85 'Vaticano', a nun's voice answers when the number 6982 is dialled. An automatic exchange was introduced into the Vatican telephone system even before the United States had one. It is important to keep up with the times. The services of a pharmacy are also provided. There is even a time-clock to ensure that punctuality is maintained.

86–88 In the fifteen years of Paul VI's pontificate, many additions were made to the Vatican. South of the basilica, near the wall, a huge Audience Hall was built by the Italian architect, Nervi. A roof garden was laid out on the roof of the Apostolic Palace and the Belvedere Court acquired new paving-stones. One always has the feeling of being in a large city. The Vigilanza direct the traffic and see to it that photographers don't manage to come too near the filling-stations and the supermarket.

89–91 A final check on proofs in the office of the editor of the Osservatore Romano. *The editor-in-chief, Valerio Volpini, and his deputy, Don Virgilio Levi, discuss last-minute corrections to the daily edition with the printers. This newspaper has been in circulation since 1851 and is responsible for spreading the word of the Pope throughout the world. The main contents of the daily Italian edition, which has a circulation of about 100,000, are compiled into weekly editions, which appear in French, English, Portuguese, Spanish and German.*

92–95 As well as its flag and coinage, the Vatican, like any other state, has its own postage stamps, which are among the most popular collectors' items in the world. Special issues often run into millions. Above: Detail from a block of provisional issues for 80 centisimi, overprinted for 40 centisimi (1934). Centre: A 2 centisimi issue from 1869. Below: Piece of an insured letter from Rome to Alexandria, dated 24 April 1869, which bears stamps to the value of 80 centisimi, the highest possible franking for that time.
Dr Plini discusses designs for new stamps with his colleagues in the Governatorato.

96–97 Pope Pius XI commissioned Guglielmo Marconi to build a radio station for the Vatican. The first papal address was broadcast to the world on 12 February 1931. During World War II, Vatican Radio was used almost exclusively for tracing imprisoned or missing soldiers and civilians. Today, 300 people from thirty-three countries work for Vatican Radio. On the air for twenty hours every day, it broadcasts a total of 500 weekly programmes in thirty-three languages to all parts of the world, on short wave, medium wave and VHF.

98–100 Built during the pontificate of Pius XI, the Vatican railway station is linked up with the Italian railway network. Nowadays, it is used solely as a loading place for goods on their way to the Nunciatures, the papal embassies throughout the world.

101 Beside the tower of Radio Vaticana on the hill above the Vatican Gardens, a gardener tends the small vegetable and fruit garden which supplies the papal household. Beans, cabbages and cucumbers grow between orange and lemon trees.

102–105 The Casina of Paul V, hidden in the greenery of the Vatican Gardens, was built by Pirro Ligorio. Today, it houses the Papal Academy of Sciences. Dating from the period of Italian Mannerism, it is made up of a small palace and a loggia, separated by a courtyard with a fountain. The small villa is often used for international conferences; here, for example, a group of prominent cancer researchers confer in 1978.

106–107 The Fontana della Galera, near the Bramante Stairs, dates from the reign of Pope Paul V and was built by Carlo Maderno. The galleon is made entirely of lead. From its hull, small cannons spurt water into the pond.

108–110 Strolling in the quiet of the Vatican Gardens, the Secretary of State, Cardinal Villot, has a pleasant chat with Cardinal Sergio Guerri from the Commission for the Vatican City and with Monsignor Casaroli, the Vatican 'foreign minister'.

111 A medieval tower marks the Casa del Giardiniere (The Gardener's House). It is here that the Commission for Archaeological Studies and Research has its headquarters. This body was set up in 1960 by John XXIII.

112 The Ukrainian Archbishop Slipyj, now living in the Vatican, reads his breviary in the quiet of the Gardens, far from the noise of the Roman traffic.

113–116 The Campo Santo Teutonico (Holy Fields of the Germans), with its College, is an enclave on Vatican soil going back to the time of Charlemagne. In the cemetery, shaded by the dome of Saint Peter, many Germano-Romans are laid to rest.

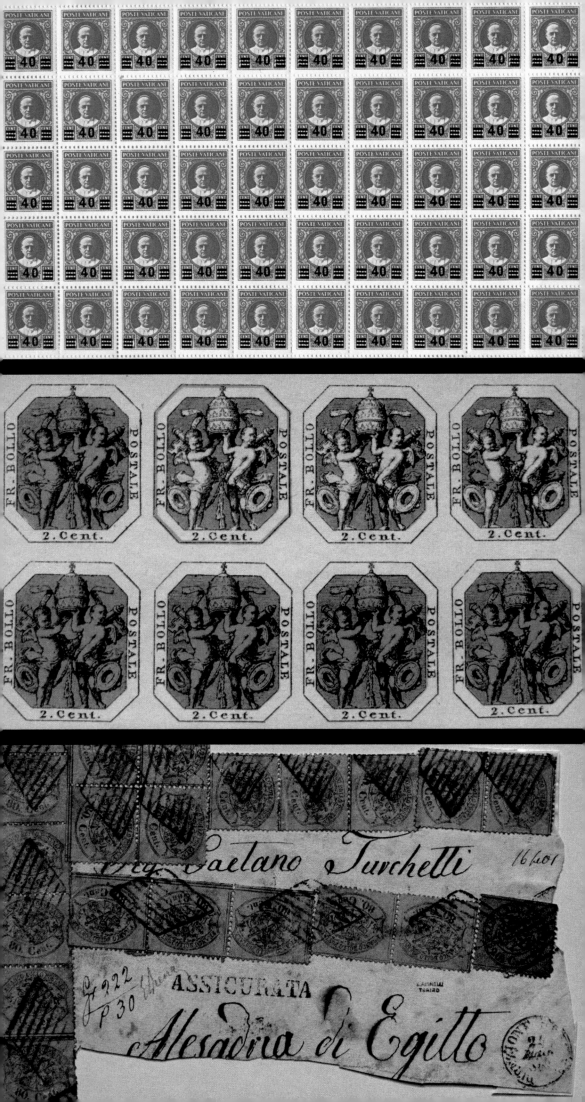

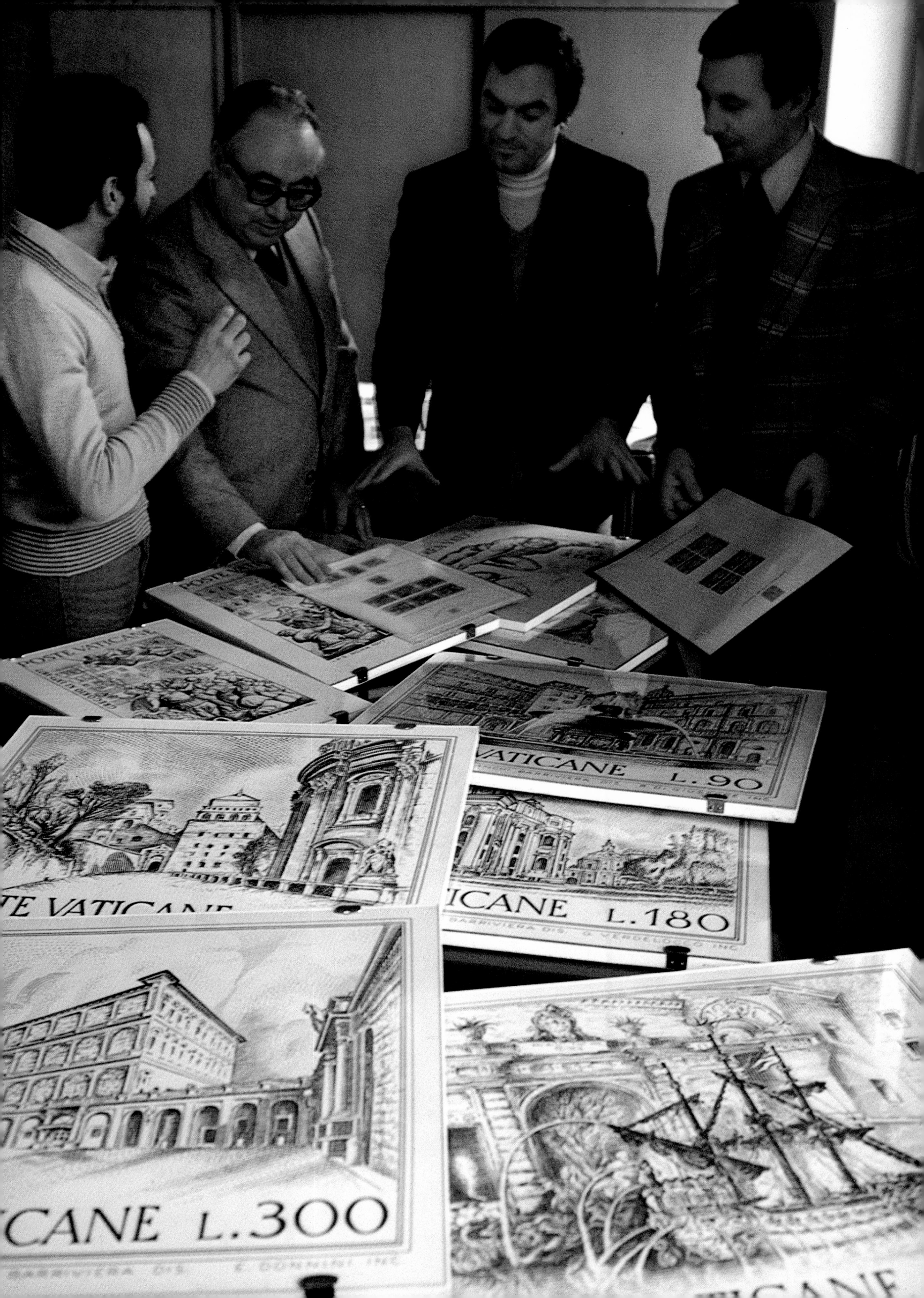
VATICANE L.90
TE VATICANE
TICANE L.180
TICANE L.300

98–100

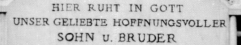

HIER RUHT IN GOTT
UNSER GELIEBTE HOFFNUNGSVOLLER
SOHN u. BRUDER

JOHANNES SKOLUD

GEB. 17·6·1906 ZU SCHWIENTOCHLOWITZ
GEST. ALS PILGER ZU ROM
AM 23·7·ANNO SANTO 1925

ZIEHET GEN ROM, WIE ICH
IN FROMMEM SINN!
IHR KOMMT, WENN GNAD EUCH WIRD,
ZU JESUS HIN.

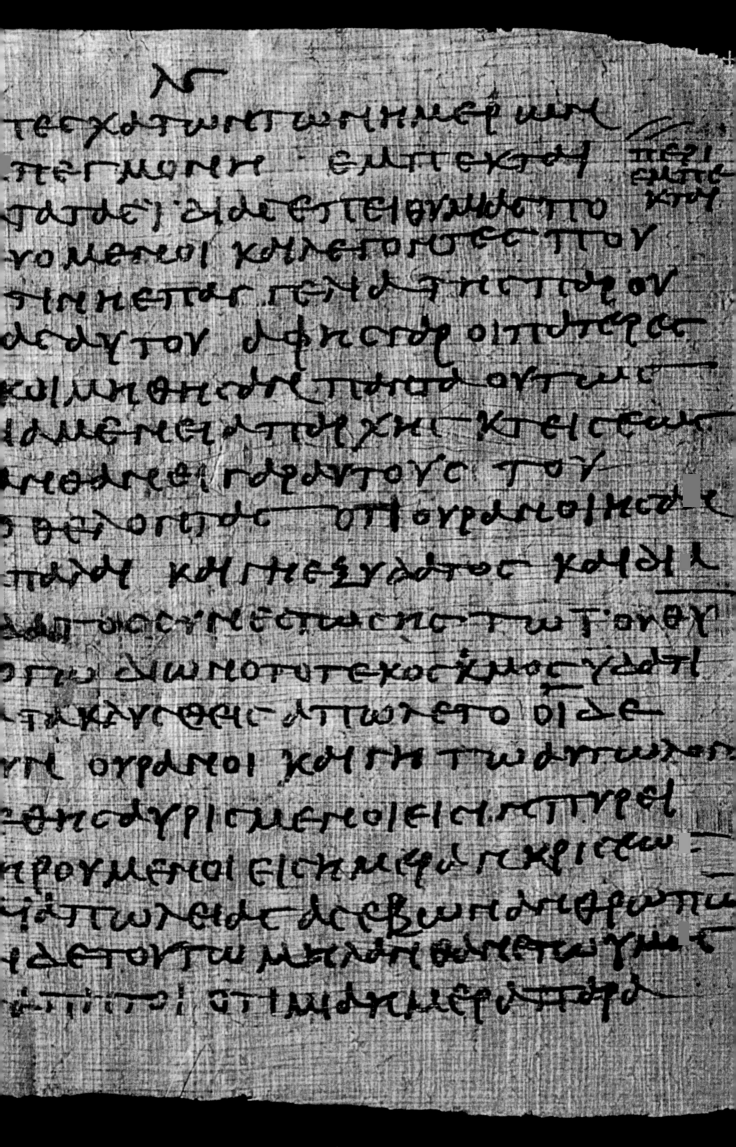

The Vatican Museums and Library

D. Redig de Campos

T he Vatican, apart from providing the customary residence of the Popes, can claim special and universal recognition in the fields of art and science by virtue of its complex of papal museums, palaces and galleries, together with the Apostolic Vatican Library. A brief article, however, permits us to deal only with the fabric of the museum and library, omitting a detailed discussion of their artistic and bibliographic treasures.

With the dawn of the Renaissance, the Vatican's museum and library—art and science in the broadest sense—were treated by the Church in different ways. Although the Middle Ages, thanks to the quiet, patient work of monastic scribes, copied and thereby preserved the written heritage of pagan antiquity, no one attempted to save the monuments and works of art left from the classical past. Especially vulnerable were the sculptures of pre-Christian Rome, many of them unique copies of famous Greek originals, long lost but recorded in historical accounts. While marble statues were broken up to make chalk, bronze castings went into the pot for melting down into weapons and bells. The *Marcus Aurelius* on the Campidoglio (the Capitol or Capitoline Hill) survived only because it was believed to be an equestrian portrait of Constantine, the first Christian Emperor. This fortunate error gave the ancient work a place of honour in front of the Popes' old Lateran Palace.

What was the reason for this disparate, indeed contradictory, attitude on the part of the Church towards the visual and literary expressions of the classical world? The explanation would seem to lie mainly in the all too evident pagan, mythological content of antique art, which, being sensuously seductive, seemed a dangerous influence on ignorant and superstitious people. Other conditions prevailed in literature, for only an educated minority could read and to them the ancient texts posed no threats, whereas a statue stood out for all to see.

Traces of this cautious, medieval mentality survived into the sixteenth century. At the very height of the Renaissance the Dutch Pope, Adrian VI (1522–23)—the last non-Italian to mount the throne of Peter until John Paul II in 1978—viewed the *Laocoön* in the Vatican's Sculpture Garden and called the famous Hellenistic group a nest of 'pagan idols'. Pius V (1566–72) donated to the Capitol and to the King of Spain a number of ancient marble masterpieces that had adorned the Vatican's Belvedere courtyard and Villa Pia because he thought them unsuitable for a papal residence!

The Museums

Late-medieval Europe's rediscovery of and passion for classical antiquity was fundamental to the cultural and economic 'rebirth' that the movement's chief spokesmen—the Tuscan humanists—called the Renaissance, meaning a revival of the high level of civilisation then thought to have flourished in antiquity before the onset of the barbarian raids. But as the Renaissance Italians attempted to imitate Greek and Roman works, they succeeded in creating a new style, which, because transfigured by Christianity, came to seem actually superior to the venerated prototypes. No longer was the study of the ancient world limited to its written heritage. Alongside the libraries arose the museums, with neither the one nor the other kept completely closed and private as the monastic libraries had been. Both visual and literary collections were opened to students, artists and connoisseurs alike.

The Octagonal Courtyard, built on the instructions of Pope Julius II (1503–13) as a Sculpture Garden. The niche in the left background contains the Laocoön.

The great humanist Pope, Sixtus IV (1471–84), responded generously to the needs of this new development. In the year of his election, he endowed the Capitol—the ancient and still active seat of the Roman Senate—with his own precious collection of antique statues, there opening modern Europe's first public museum. Moreover, Sixtus put into effect a project vainly cherished by his predecessor, Nicholas V (1447–55), when in 1475 he instituted, 'for the general convenience of learned men', the Apostolic Vatican Library, the second such collection in Europe after that founded in 1433 at Florence's Convent of Saint Mark.

Pope Julius II (1503–13), nephew of Sixtus IV, followed his uncle's example and created a museum, this time in the Vatican itself. For the collection he constructed what is now the Octagonal Courtyard, a garden enclosed within the north and east wings of Innocent III's Belvedere (the only sections built at that time). This had been set aside as a hostel for artists working on the papal palaces, among them Leonardo da Vinci.

To this Sculpture Garden Julius II contributed a signal work acquired while he was still a cardinal—the celebrated *Apollo Belvedere*. Julius believed this great marble to have been carved in Greece. Its ideal beauty exercised a profound influence on the evolution of sculpture in the sixteenth century as well as in the ages that followed, a trend that reached a climax in the neo-classical style formulated during the late eighteenth and early nineteenth centuries. In fact, the *Apollo Belvedere* proved to be only a free Roman copy made about A.D. 130 after a lost Greek bronze of the fourth century B.C.

During Julius' pontificate, the famous Sculpture Garden was adorned with other marbles, among them the *Laocoön*, the *Venus Felix*, the *Abandoned Arian Woman* (then believed to be Cleopatra) and the two recumbent personifications of the Tiber and the Nile. The designer of this open-air museum seems to have been Donato Bramante, the first architect of the new Saint Peter's. But this *hortus conclusus* of ancient art remained inaccessible to the general public, as did the Capitoline collection. Indeed, an inscription placed above the entrance advised the merely curious to keep their distance (*procul este profani*), but the admonition did not apply to genuine students and artists.

After this promising start, there followed a long period of stagnation, which continued until the second half of the eighteenth century, when the Vatican's long-dormant artistic powers awakened with the building of the impressive Pio-Clementine Museum. Absorbing the Sculpture Garden, the new structure and its collections form the essential historical nucleus of the Vatican Museums.

Here too humanism generated the revived interest in antiquity. But this late-eighteenth-century variant of an old tradition took on a rather severe, academic character, which gave birth to two new and related sciences: archaeology and art history. The father of modern archaeology was the German Johann Joachim Winckelmann (1717–68), whose *History of the Art of Antiquity* appeared in 1764. As for art history, it had its origin in Abbot Luigi Lanzi, from Treia, who in 1795–96 published his six-volume pictorial history of Italy, a rare and valuable book even today. Both these authors regarded art not only as a source of aesthetic pleasure, but also as a subject worthy of methodical or scientific study based on a comparison of the stylistic peculiarities of the various periods and the influence of one period on another. Throughout this new humanistic development the Vatican Library again backed up and supported the Museum.

Winckelmann settled in Rome in 1755 and in 1763 Clement VIII (1758–66) appointed him superintendent of antiquities. Meanwhile, the German scholar also served as advisor to Cardinal Alessandro Albani (1692–1770), who was the official Church librarian and the owner of a famous collection of antique statues, then preserved in the Villa Albani, a structure designed and built in the years 1746–63 by Carlo Marchionni.

Before the construction of the so-called Pio-Clementine galleries, the Vatican's collections were housed in a variety of minor museums, all under the authority of the Vatican Library. Among these was the Galleria Lapidaria, devoted to ancient funerary inscriptions, both pagan and Christian, with the latter derived mainly from the catacombs. Assembled by order of Benedict XIV (1740–58), the Lapidaria first found a home on the north side of the east wing of the Bramante corridor and later, under Pius VII (1800–23), in its present location on the south side of the same corridor, there installed by the famous epigrapher Gaetano Marini. Also in the time of Benedict XIV came the Museo Sacro ('Sacred Museum'), founded 'to increase the splendour of the city and to assert the truth of holy religion'. This made it a resource for the study of early Church history. Housed at the south side of the western wing of the Bramante corridor, the Sacro materials were placed under the care of Francesco Vettori, a rich collector who donated some 6,500 pieces of ancient jewellery to the Sacro collection. Also not to be overlooked are the Vatican coin cabinets, despite their depletion by Napoleon, who after the Treaty of Tolentino (1797) moved the collection to Paris. Finally, there is the Museo Profano ('Profane Museum') initiated by Clement XIII and built in a space on the north side of the corridor's west wing, near the Quattro Cancelli ('Four Chancels') entrance. The director was to have been Winckelmann had the great writer not been murdered in Trieste in 1768.

Once completed during the reign of Pius VI, the Sacred and Profane Museums became the home of some two hundred Greek and Etruscan vases belonging to Cardinal Gualtieri, the Albani coins, and the Carpegna gems, cameos, ivories and bronzes. These works, like the funerary inscriptions, had been found in Rome's catacombs. Clement XIII and Benedict XIV built the collection, acquiring the gems through the Vettori bequest just mentioned.

In accord with his wishes, Winckelmann was succeeded in his Vatican post by Giovanni Antonio Battista Visconti (1722–84), who had been his mentor's disciple since the age of fourteen. Scarcely had the new director taken office when he encountered the mounting problem of overcrowding in the Vatican Museums, a problem that became his specific responsibility. At best, the accommodations made for many of the papal holdings proved inadequate. Further aggravating the situation were laws restricting the exportation of newly excavated antiquities. The laws applied most specifically to the Mattei and Fusconi collections and to such famous statues as the so-called *Chastity*, the *Eros of Centocelle* and the *Running Girl*. Owing to the legislation, these works could be placed neither in the Vatican nor in the Capitoline Museum.

The decision to create a museum and make it an entity separate from the collections of the Apostolic Library was taken by Clement XIV (1769–74), acting on the advice of the Visconti family and on that of the Cardinal Treasurer, Giovanni Angelo Braschi, who succeeded to the Chair of Peter as Pius VI (1775–99). Placed under the supervision of architects Alessandro Dori (d. 1772), Michelangelo Simonetti (1724–87), and Giulio Camporese (1754–1840), construction got under way in 1771 and concluded in 1773, but the work consisted mainly of adapting older buildings rather than putting up new ones. What the campaign created includes the present Sculpture Gallery (badly situated in the gallery of Innocent VIII's *palazzina*, where the arrangement has partially obliterated the frescoes of Pinturicchio); the Hall of Animals, modified from a sixteenth-century structure; and the rather baroque transformation of the old Sculpture Garden, which Simonetti, after succeeding Dori in 1772, made into the Octagonal Courtyard. In the four arches of the portico stand the *Apollo Belvedere*, the *Laocoön*, the *Hermes* attributed to Praxiteles, the *Two Boxers* and the *Perseus* of Antonio Canova.

The new complex became known as the Clementine Museum, even though the limited scope of the structural work made it automatically obsolete as a space for the vast amount of art to be displayed. Thus, Angelo Braschi had scarcely been elected Pope (1775) when he determined to resolve the problem once and for all by commissioning an entirely new museum, consisting of structures created and designed exclusively for this purpose.

Pius VI entrusted the task to Michelangelo Simonetti, with Camporese as his assistant. Work began in 1776—with an act of mindless vandalism! To extend the Sculpture Gallery by some ten metres, the architects destroyed the chapel of Innocent VIII's *palazzina*, leaving not a trace of Andrea Mantegna's decorations, a cycle so admired by Clement XIV that he had only just restored it! Then to join the various library museums to the Clementine Museum, Simonetti introduced his great staircase, a masterpiece that, owing to its transitional, late-baroque style, almost escapes notice as a work of late-eighteenth century neo-classical Rome. This staircase, with its decorations painted in the style of Tiepolo, leads to three vast halls, all adjacent to one another but each built to a different plan. They are the Hall of the Greek Cross, the Rotonda Hall

This figure, one of the family group of Julius Claudius, stands in the Museo Profano.

The Rotonda Hall is part of the eighteenth-century Pio-Clementine Museum.

(whose shallow dome and oculus derive from Rome's second-century Pantheon), and the Hall of the Muses, in the centre of which the *Belvedere Torso* stands under a vault frescoed by Tommaso Conca. At this point the museum becomes a single complex, by means of the Hall of Animals, which links the new construction to the Clementine rooms. Until 1932 visitors entered through the Atrium of Four Chancels at the top of the Stradone dei Musei, a square one-storey building containing the circular Chariot Room, completed in 1784 by Giulio Camporese.

The so-called Pio-Clementine buildings were inaugurated in 1787, just ten years before their most precious contents were transferred to Paris as war booty exacted by Napoleon under terms of the Treaty of Tolentino. After the Battle of Waterloo, the Congress of Vienna (1815) decreed that the papal treasures should all be returned to Rome, where they arrived in the time of Pius VII (1800–23).

It now fell to Antonio Canova, the great neo-classical sculptor who had been made Rome's Inspector of Fine Arts, to resolve two problems: the exhibition of works acquired to fill the gaps left by the Napoleonic seizure, and the proper display of the most famous of the paintings returned from France. For the pictures, a solution came with the decision not to rehang the works as before, but rather to place them on exhibition in a special gallery that would be open to the general public. This very select collection would include three masterpieces by Raphael: the *Coronation of the Virgin*, transferred from Perugia's San Francesco d'Assisi; the *Madonna del Foligno*, also formerly in Perugia, at the Convent of Saint Anne; and the *Transfiguration*, a late painting once in the apse of Rome's San Pietro in Montorio.

To deal with the new sculptures, Canova commissioned a new wing, placing the work in the hands of the Roman architect Raffaele Stern (1774–1820), who designed a large barrel-vaulted hall with skylights and wall niches. The structure closed the south side of the Cortile della Pigna. Among the well-known statues placed there are the *Augustus of Primaporta*, the *Goldbearer*, the *Wounded Amazon* (copied from a work of Polykleitos), the *Nile*, and the stupendous figure of *Demosthenes*, unusually realistic for a Greek work. Opened in 1822, the new wing with its deliberate severity of style typifies neo-classical taste.

Canova moved busts, pillars, sarcophagi, and other minor works to the adjacent north side of the east wing of the Bramante corridor, there installing them in a space known as the Chiaramonte Museum. The arrangement resembles nothing so much as a well-organised department store, which means that it lacks any great museological interest.

Meanwhile, the Borgia apartments served as a depot for the main papal collection, which consisted of the pictures recovered from Paris and other works from the Sacred Palaces. The collection then passed through various Vatican apartments, increasing in value as it went, and finally came to rest in a building commissioned by Pius XI (1922–39). Designed by Luca Beltrami, the facility opened to the public in 1932.

Gregory XIII (1831–46) founded the Gregorian-Etruscan Museum in 1837 and the Gregorian-Egyptian Museum in 1839, thereby expanding the Vatican museums well beyond their original concentration on Graeco-Roman antiquities. The new displays were mounted in rooms set aside on the first and second floors of the building that constitutes the south wing of the Octagonal Courtyard. In 1844 the same Pope established the Museo Profano Lateranense on the ground floor of the Lateran Palace, which later received two further collections: the Christian Museum in 1854 and the Missionary-Ethnographic Museum in 1926. It was these three collections that John XXIII (1958–63) brought together in the Vatican itself, there installed in a new and totally modern building which in 1971 opened its doors as the Pauline Wing, built from plans by Vincenzo Passarelli. Besides the three collections already mentioned, the Pauline Wing also included the new 'Historical Museum', composed of papal carriages and the arms, uniforms, standards, and other memorabilia of the papal military forces. Also from the nineteenth century is the Gallery of Candelabra, opened in 1883 by Leo XIII (1878–1903) for the Vatican's collection related to pagan archaeology.

The most recent galleries to be opened in the Vatican Museums are those established by Paul VI for the display of his collection of modern religious art. They occupy a sequence of spaces that include the restored Borgia apartments and even the basement of the Sistine Chapel. The collection numbers some 740 works, all of them by twentieth-century masters. Inaugurated in 1973, this new addition affirms the Church's traditional concern for art.

Although they form part of the Vatican Museums, the famous rooms and chapels of the papal palace do not function as exhibition space. Being magnificently frescoed, they naturally contain some of the greatest art works owned by the Vatican. Among the finest of these wall cycles are those by Fra Angelico in the chapels of Nicholas V, the vaults painted in the Borgia apartments by Pinturicchio and his school, and, of course, the colossal decorative programmes spread over the surfaces of the Sistine Chapel, which Perugino, Botticelli, Ghirlandaio, Signorelli, Cosimo Rosselli, and Michelangelo transformed into one of the supreme marvels of human achievement. Then in the Gallery of Saint Damasus are the works of Raphael and his school. Altogether, the wall decorations make the Vatican the largest museum of frescoes in the world.

The Vatican Museums can also be looked upon as a museum of museography—a laboratory devoted to the scientific search for the ideal environment in which to enjoy, study, conserve, and exhibit works of art. Such a search never occurred to the 'antiquaries' who arranged the Sculpture Garden, since their concern was to save the most precious antiquities from the weather by placing them in Bramante's niches and alcoves. It was never anything but a garden, arranged with a gardener's sense of order and populated by marble gods without temples.

In the Pio-Clementine buildings, Simonetti and Comporese tried to strike a balance between architectural realities and artistic-archaeological requirements. There the statues could be rearranged (and often have been) without spoiling the effect. But the Hall of the Muses seems to have been designed for the specific purpose of providing the *Belvedere Torso* with better illumination. Room and statue complement one another in a museum that embodies the harmonious vision of the eighteenth century.

The new section that Stern built for Canova marked an important step in the evolution of the modern museum. It was here that architecture came to be recognised as the true companion of archaeology and art history. Compared with the Pio-Clementine buildings, the new structure has a distinct aesthetic character, which emerges directly from its function as a museum. Rather than a suite of palace rooms, the spaces are such that they would be meaningless without the sculptures that fill them.

The Pauline Wing constitutes the Vatican's latest step in the process of museological evolution. Putting into effect Le Corbusier's conception of the museum as *une machine à exposer*, the Pauline Wing brings the Vatican into the forefront of modern museum design. Its totally modernistic style, both in the permanent structure and in its moveable metal parts, provides a dramatically contrasted and therefore effective context for the display of antique sculptures. Designed for sculpture, the galleries, thanks to their flexible equipment, can be arranged at will and reinstalled with totally different works.

The total area covered by the Vatican Museums is over 40,000 square yards, with wall space extending to almost five miles! The average number of daily visitors is 5,000, a number that increases all the time. A peak was reached in Holy Year, 1975, when the Museums opened their doors to 16,000 souls almost daily. The staff maintaining the buildings numbers 197, including directors, manager, technicians, security and janitorial personnel. At present the museums are divided up into the following departments: Oriental Antiquity; Medieval; Modern and Byzantine Art; Paleo-Christian Art; Epigraphic Collection; Ethnological Collection; Collection of Contemporary Religious Art; Restoration Laboratories (founded by Pius XI in 1922); and Scientific Research. It was the last two departments that achieved the remarkable restoration of Michelangelo's *Pietà*, after the hammer-blows given it by a deranged man visiting Saint Peter's in 1972. This tragic and unique incident made the world community once again keenly aware of the priceless treasures contained and beautifully preserved in the sovereign city of the Popes.

The Library

Before sketching the five-hundred-year history of the Apostolic Vatican Library, we must contrast it with the earlier collections of books and documents safeguarded by the Church. For example, there was the Lateran *scrinium*, recorded in the fourth century under Pope Saint Silvester (314–335); then came the library of Pope Boniface VIII

The Belvedere Torso *in the Hall of the Muses, one of the many rooms in the Pio-Clementine complex.*

Part of the storage section in the Vatican Secret Archives.

(1294–1303), which lasted into the Avignon era (1309–77). These 'papal libraries' were for the use of the Pope and the Curia only, which left the collections closed to the public. Manuscripts, almost exclusively ecclesiastical, legal or historical, could be consulted, especially during the councils, but not used for study.

The Vatican Library, on the other hand, was modelled on the library of San Marco at Florence (1444), which made it a 'humanist' library, open to all 'learned men' and a source of documentation for all the intellectual disciplines cultivated by the Renaissance. Indeed, it was the idea of a humanist Pope: Tommaso Parentucelli of Sarzana, who became Nicholas V (1447–55). 'It was said,' wrote Vespasiano da Bisticci, 'that if ever [Parentucelli] had any money to hand, he would spend it on two things—books and buildings.' In fact, although he was never rich, this future Pope bought—or had copied for him—manuscripts of every kind, and thus compiled a notable private library which he brought with him to Rome, there entrusting it to the care of the humanist Giovanni Tortelli. When he died in 1455, Nicholas V's library contained 800 Latin and 353 Greek codices. Another fifty-six were found in his bedroom, which adjoined the room where he had temporarily left his books.

This was the nucleus of the future Vatican Library, which the Pontiff had dreamt of as 'a large and roomy hall, lit with windows on the side walls, for the common use of the studious'. In other words, it was meant to be a proper public library. Nicholas left no indication as to where such a building might be constructed, but ideas for it must have been considered somewhere among his impressive building plans. Conceived by Leon Battista Alberti and described by Giannozzo Manetti, the projects of the Pope included the completion of the papal palaces, begun under Nicholas III (1277–80) but abandoned when the papal court removed to Avignon in 1309.

Nicholas built and wrote incessantly, as Vespasiano da Bisticci records. During the plague of 1450, the Pope went to Fabriano (where the best paper was made), 'but neither builders nor writers and translators who were left behind stopped their work: what he had begun was continued without interruption.' The enormous task 'would have been a remarkable piece of work, had it been achieved, but he was prevented by death from completing it.'

With the death of Nicholas V on 24 March 1455, the projects sponsored by this Pope were stopped and no more was heard of the Vatican Library. Little or no progress occurred under Callistus III (1455–58) and Pius II (1458–64). Although a fervent humanist, the latter occupied himself solely with his own personal library. Nor was Paul II (1464–71) any more active in regard to Nicholas V's dream. Only with the arrival of Sixtus IV (1471–84) did work recommence, after sixteen years. By then, the number of Latin and Greek codices owned by the Vatican Library had risen to a total of 2,527, of which 824 had been bequeathed by Pope Nicholas.

When Giovanni Andrea Bussi, 'guardian' of the papal library, died on 4 February in the Holy Year 1475, the Pope appointed as his successor the humanist Bartolomeo Sacchi, known as 'Platina', with the same title and duties as Bussi. He was assisted by Demetrio Guazzelli, who had been a fellow member of the Roman Academy of Pomponio Leto (an organisation that incurred the disapproval of Paul II). It looked as if nothing would change, but Sixtus IV had other ideas. With the Bull *Ad Decorem Militantis Ecclesiae* of 15 June 1475, this Pope formally founded the Apostolic Vatican Library, provided the funds the collection required and placed it under the direction of Platina, who now became the 'governor and guardian' of the new institution—a title equivalent in modern terms to 'director'.

In the Vatican, rooms were set aside for the library on the ground floor of the north wing of the Cortile del Pappagallo, onto which they opened. Its western part built by Nicholas V, this structure constituted one of the first examples of Florentine Renaissance architecture in Rome. It was the work of Antonio di Francesco of Florence, together with Rossellino, the 'papal engineer' of the time. Until invested with the library, the building had been used as a canteen and granary. It consists of a succession of four adjoining vaulted rooms, which, from west to east, came to be known as the Latin Library, the Greek Library (which with the Latin Library formed the Common Library, open to all students), the Secret Library (which contained the more precious manuscripts and offered more limited access), and finally, from 1480, the Library of Popes. The largest of the four, this last collection is housed in a room of the palace of Boniface VIII, which then could boast a splendid new vault. Here are kept the secret archives and the *regesta*. It should be noted that the Vatican archives were originally connected to the Library and became detached from it only in 1630.

The work of adapting the architecture to the needs of the Library began on 30 June 1475, only fifteen days after the investiture of Platina in his new office. The walls that had divided the future Latin Library into six small rooms were demolished and artists began decorating the new interior on 29 November of that year. Among them were such well-known figures as Melozzo da Forlì, Antoniazzo Romano, Domenica and David del Ghirlandaio. The Ghirlandaio brothers frescoed the vaults of the Latin Library with two great armorial devices of the Church and with two more representing the oak-trees of Sixtus IV. No doubt it was David, the more modest of the two, who did most of the work. In the twelve skylights and on the edges of the vaults, thickly decorated with oak-wreaths in chiaroscuro, the artistic team painted frescoes portraying six fathers of the Latin Church and six learned men from ancient Greece. The figures appear as half-busts, seen from the front behind window-sills, each of them holding a scroll with an epithet written on it.

On the north wall, between two windows, Melozzo da Forlì painted the solemn audience granted by the Pope to Platina on the occasion of his investiture. With its intense vitality and grandiose perspective, this fresco is one of the artist's finest works. It dates from the years 1475–77. Removed from the wall about 1820 and mounted on canvas, the painting now hangs in the Vatican picture-gallery. Melozzo's assistant for this work was Antoniazzo Romano.

Next door, the Greek Library may be compared with the Sala del Mappamondo in Rome's Palazzo Venezia (1455), the work of an unknown artist from the school of Mantegna. It is decorated with a simulated architectural work, consisting of multi-coloured columns and classical friezes, surmounted by balustraded skylights and flower-vases decorated with streamers. Human figures are absent, except above the west window, where two men appear above the lintel, in half-bust profile: the older one on the right, wearing a voluminous veil over his head; the younger one on the left with a wreath about his hair. Perhaps they are meant to symbolise a master with his apprentice. Both pictures are reminiscent of the style of Antoniazzo. At the centre of the two vaults above this room are two coats of arms, apparently identical: gold keys crossed on a crimson field, surmounted by a tiara. The one facing the Cortile del Pappagallo constitutes the escutcheon of the Church, adopted by Nicholas V. The other is identical to the first but distinguished by the letters N.PP.V. written, contrary to heraldic usage, in the lower part of the field. If the Greek and Latin Libraries were decorated in the same years—as the abundance of oak-wreaths in both would seem to indicate—the surprising presence of the escutcheon of Nicholas V in this room cannot be explained except as a loyal sign of recognition by Sixtus IV of his predecessor's achievements, which included the initial concept of the Vatican Library now realised.

Another hypothesis—justifiable but less likely—dates the paintings in this room to the pontificate of Nicholas, when the space was used for private audiences and other minor ceremonies. But the presence of the two figures of master and apprentice, though perhaps appropriate in a library, cannot be explained in such a context. Moreover, no trace has been found during recent restoration work of any decoration applied to the edges of the vault or the skylights previous to (or different from) the actual wreath-motif that survives. In the absence of conclusive evidence, the question remains open. As for the frescoes, they could be the creation of Melozzo da Forlì, a great master of the new science of optical perspective, but executed in a rather workmanlike manner by his assistant Antoniazzo Romano.

Nothing remains of the Secret Library's original decoration which had been executed by Melozzo and Antoniazzo. According to an eighteenth-century record of Chattard, this room was 'completely covered by tables, including the vault'. This must refer to painted panels and niches, for the two artists were paid by Platina on 30 June 1478 'for the painting done in the Secret Library and in the (Papal) Library recently annexed'. The restoration of 1967 rediscovered and completed the rare

The salone *of Sixtus V (1585–90). This great hall, with its two aisles over 200 feet long and fifty feet wide, is the main exhibition area in the Vatican Library.*

and elegant pictorial decoration of the vault, which comprises stylised grey foliage on a white background. The room, considerably larger than the others, was incorporated in the Vatican a few days before Platina died of the plague on 28 December 1481.

The furnishing of the Library is depicted in a contemporary fresco in the Ospedale di Santo Spirito, which shows Sixtus IV visiting the Vatican. Part of the pulpits and veneered desks can be seen today in the vestibule of the new site provided for the Library by Sixtus V at the end of the sixteenth century. As in Florence's Library, the codices were chained to the reading-desks, but from the time of Platina until 1556, they were—incredibly—available on loan! Hardly less remarkable is the fact that this furniture was designed by Giovannino dei Dolci, the architect of the Sistine Chapel.

The Vatican Library remained as first installed for little more than a century, from 1478 until 1587, whereupon Sixtus V (1585–90) opened a second facility. The change occurred for many reasons: too little space to accommodate the expanding number of acquisitions, the dampness of the buildings and not least the increasing activity of presses since the invention of mechanical printing in 1455. The latter phenomenon arose despite the objections of humanists of the old school like Vespasiano da Bisticci, who nostalgically described the famous library of the bibliophile prince, Federico, duke of Urbino, as one in which 'all the books are superbly beautiful, all hand-written, without one printed copy to bring shame on it. . . .' This was the spirit in which the first Vatican Library had been conceived, with no thought of what wondrous inventions the future would bring.

The complex of buildings of which the fifteenth-century Vatican formed part made it impossible to extend in any direction. By the reign of Sixtus V, the problem had become acute, which prompted the Pope to initiate the construction of an entirely new building—larger, drier, with better lighting, and capable of extension into the Papal Palace. Sixtus entrusted the work to his favourite architect, Domenico Fontana. The structure was to be erected in the Cortile di Belvedere, where the grand staircase leading to the first of the two north-facing terraces had once stood, between the two pavilions added by Pirro Ligorio to the two long corridors designed by Bramante in 1503.

Work began in May 1587 and ended successfully just over a year later. The entrance was in the present Galleria Lapidaria. Although subsequently much altered, the front, which overlooked the Cortile di Belvedere, is known both from contemporary prints and from a minute description by Fontana. The building itself has a ground floor with a balcony at the height of the small windows under the vaults. The mezzanine is closed, because while it once served for *scriptores*, the space now functions as the Catalogue Room. Two floors upstairs, both with rectangular windows, have been transformed into the Reading Room and the Exhibition Room. Finally, there is the famous *salone* of Sixtus V together with its eastern extension (the old Writing Room) and its western extension (the so-called 'gallery'), constructed under Pius IV (1559–65). All these rooms were vaulted and frescoed. Above the central arch of the portico, an inscription records the Pope who built it and the year of its construction: 1558. In the middle of the cornice appears the coat of arms of Sixtus V surmounted by a tiara. The original versions of both were lost when five buttresses were built into the façade in the eighteenth century. To furnish the *salone*, the Pope wanted to make use of the furniture of the old library, while the guardian, Federico Ranaldi, would have preferred to replace the medieval shelves with more suitable bookcases. These eventually came in 1645 and they remain today, despite the questionable taste of the painting done in the time of Pius IX.

It is said that the walls, vaults and pilasters of the Library were covered with frescoes painted by a hundred artists (just as there had been a hundred builders), working from a sophisticated iconographic programmed devised by Ranaldi, Silvio Antoniano and others. This took as its theme the triumph of the book down through the centuries and into the pontificate of the reigning Pope. The great wall frescoes depict the famous libraries of the ancient world and the ecumenical councils, while the pilasters bear various alphabets, with Adam, the first intelligent being, portrayed on the first pilaster and the figure of Christ—the Way, the Truth and the Life—on the last, standing between a Pope and an Emperor. Finally, plaques show the many building enterprises of Sixtus V.

Visually pleasing pictures of high quality, these works are also very important for studying the topography and history of sixteenth-century Rome. The vault is completely covered with compositions containing graceful, statuesque figures. Like the entire 'programme', these collective works were distributed among the various artists who laboured valiantly to translate ideas into images. Baglione writes that Giovanni Guerra, leader of the team of painters together with Cesare Nebbia, 'researched the historical subjects to be depicted and Cesare designed them'. It was an old-fashioned, craftsmanlike way of proceeding, even if among those hundred artists there were many, like Orazio Gentileschi, Paolo Bril, Antonio Tempesta, Ventura Salimbene and others, who already enjoyed considerable fame. Sixtus V authorised the cost of their work in 1589. By the time the books were transferred to their new home between 1590 and 1591, the painting had been completed, making the Library interiors the prime example of Roman decorative Mannerism in its second phase.

Ranaldi's programme for the sixteenth-century decorations reveals less interest in humanist motifs than had been evinced in Platina's designs for the old library. The influence of the Council of Trent was being felt. But the paintings in the two so-called Pauline Rooms (a section of the Library's western 'corridor' adjoining the great Sistine Room) reflect an apparent attempt to re-establish the humanist compromise. Here the decorative programme came from the 'vice-guardian', Alessandro Ranaldi (nephew of Federico), working under the patronage of Paul V (1605–21), who wished to preserve the private library of Giulio Orsini.

Thanks to Sixtus V, the Vatican Library had acquired a worthy and permanent resting-place. But the recurrent problem of space would require internal modifications and extension into other parts of the Vatican complex, albeit without altering its historic arrangement. Eventually, the extensions, which were intended to promote the accumulation and better conservation of the library's manuscripts and printed matter, came to be of such proportions that one can truthfully speak of a third Vatican Library, that of Leo XIII (1878–1903), who had specifically wanted a 'third library' and had the foresight to create it. Before his pontificate, the few students admitted worked in the beautiful but poorly lit Old Writers' Room (or Vestibule) and the ever-growing quantity of books piled up in the Borgia apartments.

In 1890, the opening of a shop and a Readers' Room (for printed volumes) on the floor beneath the great Sistine Room signalled the beginning of reorganisation, which was entrusted to the Jesuit Franz Ehrle, a future Prefect of the Vatican and later the Cardinal Librarian, who was particularly attentive to the historical and artistic value of the place in which he worked. Since then, work has continued almost without interruption, making the Vatican Library one of the most modern and best equipped in the world. It is worth recording the contribution made by the Prefects Achille Ratti (later Pope Pius XI, 1922–39) and Eugène Tisserant, who became Cardinal Librarian. The French prelate ordered the replacement of the old wooden furniture with over 3,000 yards of modern metal shelving; he also created the new and vast Catalogue Room beneath the Reading Room. Space precludes more than a mention of the School of Librarianship and the School of Paleography and Diplomacy (a dependent of the Secret Archives), which confers an internationally respected diploma, or the photographic facilities, the restoration laboratories, the Magazine Room and other services provided for the convenience of students.

The Library contains some 65,000 manuscripts, excluding the 130,000 documents in the archives. Printed volumes, among them 7,000 incunabula, number more than 700,000, a total that swells by some 8,000 units every year, including reviews and publications of various kinds. The admission passes issued to qualified researchers from some fifty nations numbered 2,365 between 1973 and 1974. Finally, there is *Studi e Testi*, a renowned series of learned articles, which published its two hundred and seventy-second volume in 1973 with a typical piece of research on the history of the collections and resources of the Vatican from Sixtus IV to Pius XI. Written by Jeanne Bignami Odier, with assistance from Monsignor José Ruysschaert, Vice-Prefect of the Library, this publication provides a valuable source of information from which much data for the present article have been drawn.

It has been said of the Papal Museums that they constitute a sort of museum of museology, thanks to the great care taken to change as little

A corner of the Apostolic Library of Leo XIII (1878–1903).

as possible in the traditional appearance of the buildings and their contents. These are 'classical texts' in their own right. And the same can be said of the Vatican Library, which after centuries continues to acquire and conserve in their original order whole collections and archives of such illustrious families as the Ottoboni, Chigi, Reginense, Barberini, Palatino and others, thereby enriching the original stock of the Greek and Latin Libraries. From the time of Platina, the Vatican Library has been a veritable library of libraries. Sixtus IV would indeed have been proud of the 'four libraries in one'.

The Vatican, an international centre, offers yet another advantage, that of being in a certain sense a permanent scientific meeting-place. Albeit without schedules or programmes, it serves as a common ground for personal contacts and a forum of exchange between researchers in similar fields—a matter of some importance, given the ever-growing interdependence among the different branches of modern science.

In conclusion, the Apostolic Vatican Library remains, even nowadays, a collection of manuscripts whose principal interest lies in the fields of humanist studies and church history. The specific purpose of the great Reading Room is to provide every assistance needed by serious scholars and to publish critical editions of manuscripts.

Above all, the Vatican Library adheres to the important purpose ordained for it by Sixtus IV in his famous Bull of 15 June 1475, when the great humanist Pope announced that he wanted to found a public library 'for the glory of the Church militant, for the dissemination of the Catholic faith, for the assistance and honour of the learned and the lettered'.

---

117 Among the precious objects in the treasuries of the Vatican Library are the Bodmer Papyri, the oldest existing manuscripts of the letters of Saint Peter. The Swiss collector, Martin Bodmer, presented them to Paul VI in 1969, as a gift for the Library.

118 The famous group, the Laocoön, *was excavated from the Domus Aurea of Nero near the Colosseum in 1506 and was one of the main influences on Renaissance sculpture. It was only in recent times, however, that the inaccurate reconstruction of the Greek original (the right arm) was corrected in the light of new discoveries. Today, the work stands in its original state in the Octagonal Courtyard of the Pio-Clementine Museum.*

119 Anyone who manages to find the entrance to the Vatican Museums, on the northern side of the surrounding walls, is led up the imposing winding double staircase into the never-ending labyrinth of the collections.

120 The Museo Chiaramonti was decorated by the sculptor Canova after 1800, during the pontificate of Pius VII, whose name it bears. In its accumulation of neo-classical gods and emperors, urns and sarcophagi, it differs entirely from the more modern museums of antiquities and Early Christian art, which are situated behind the art gallery.

121–122 Keeping watch over the treasures of the Museums, which, on average, are visited by 5,000 people per day, requires the efficiency of a well-oiled machine. Museum attendants, each equipped with a walkie-talkie, are within easy reach of even the most outlying rooms. They are in constant communication with a central control, which patrols the Museums by means of twenty-six closed-circuit TV monitors.

123 In the restoration laboratory under the art gallery, pictures from the collections and frescoes from the palaces are restored.

*124–125 The sisters in the 'Studio Arazzi' have no need to complain of having too little to do. Gobelins and tapestries are in constant need of repair.
Inset: Working on a Gobelin in the restoration laboratory.*

126 The Vatican secret archives were first set up by Pope Paul V. The rooms which house the archives today are the original ones which were decorated and furnished in his reign, at the beginning of the seventeenth century. The archives are accessible only to researchers with a special permit.

127 In June 1654, Queen Christina of Sweden had to give up the throne because she became a Catholic. Her abdication was recorded on this document with all its accompanying seals. Each of the 306 members of the Swedish parliament signed the document and affixed it with his red lacquer seal.

128–131 Rare books often arrive at the restoration workshops of the Vatican Library in extremely bad condition. The pages are carefully separated, each is cleaned, mounted, retouched and finally the book is rebound. Many a treasure which might have been lost has been saved in these workshops.

132–133 The Vatican Library contains more than 700,000 books. Set out in a row, the books would cover a distance of over twelve miles. Particular rarities are to be found among the 65,000 manuscripts and in the 130,000 bundles of archive material. This Jacobite Gospel from the year 1200 originally came from Ethiopia.

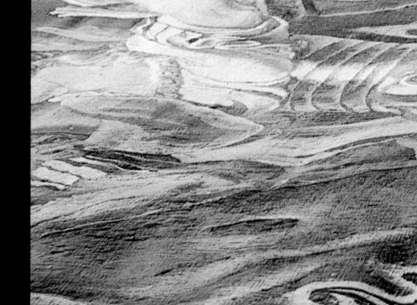

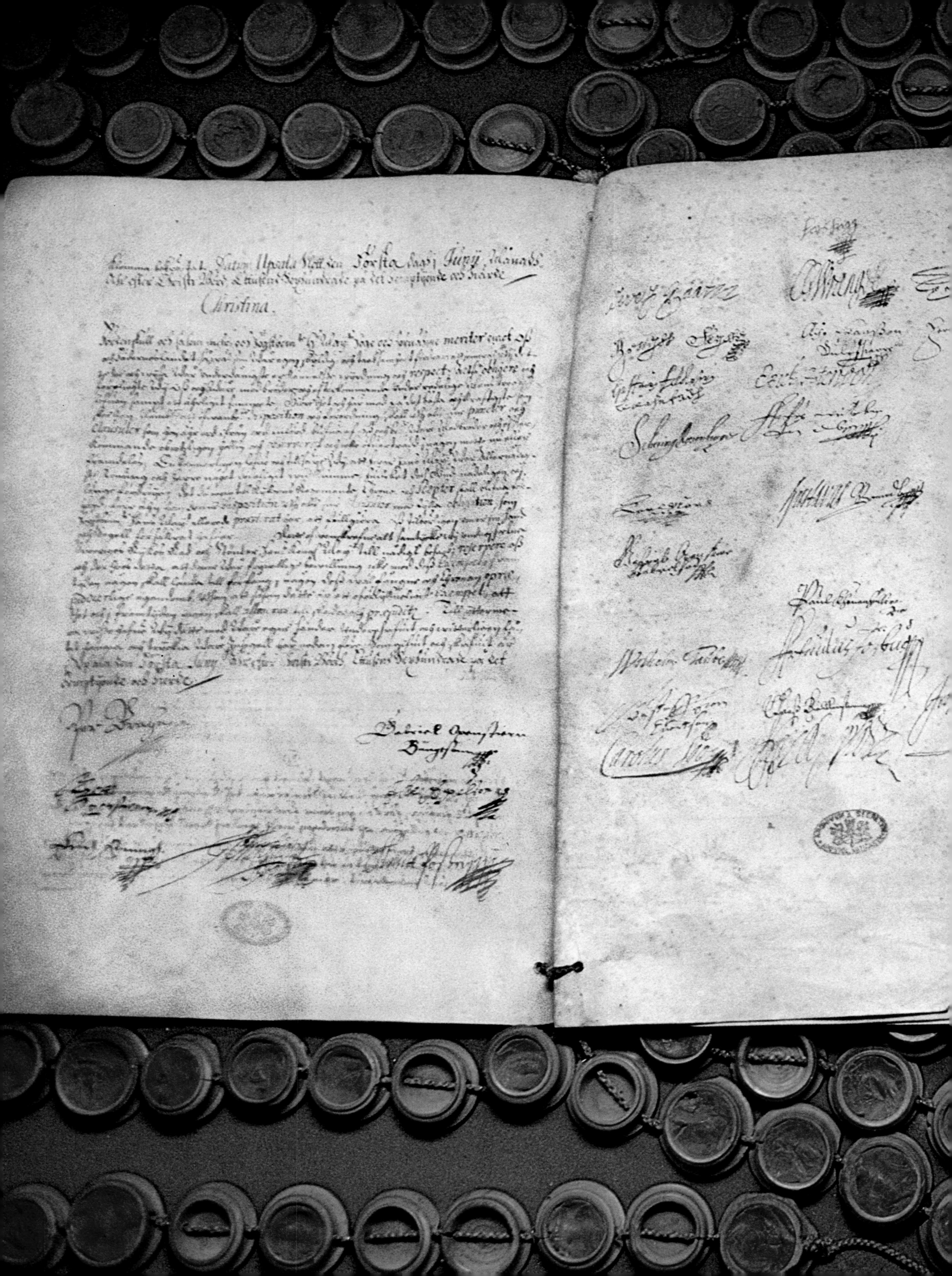

Datum Upsala Slott den Förste dagj Junij Månads
åhr efter Christi födh i tusend Sexhundrade på det örtijonde och fierde

Christina.

[handwritten body text, largely illegible Swedish chancery script]

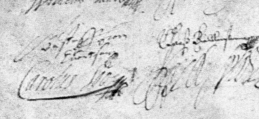

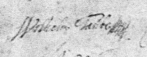

Gabriel Oxenstiern

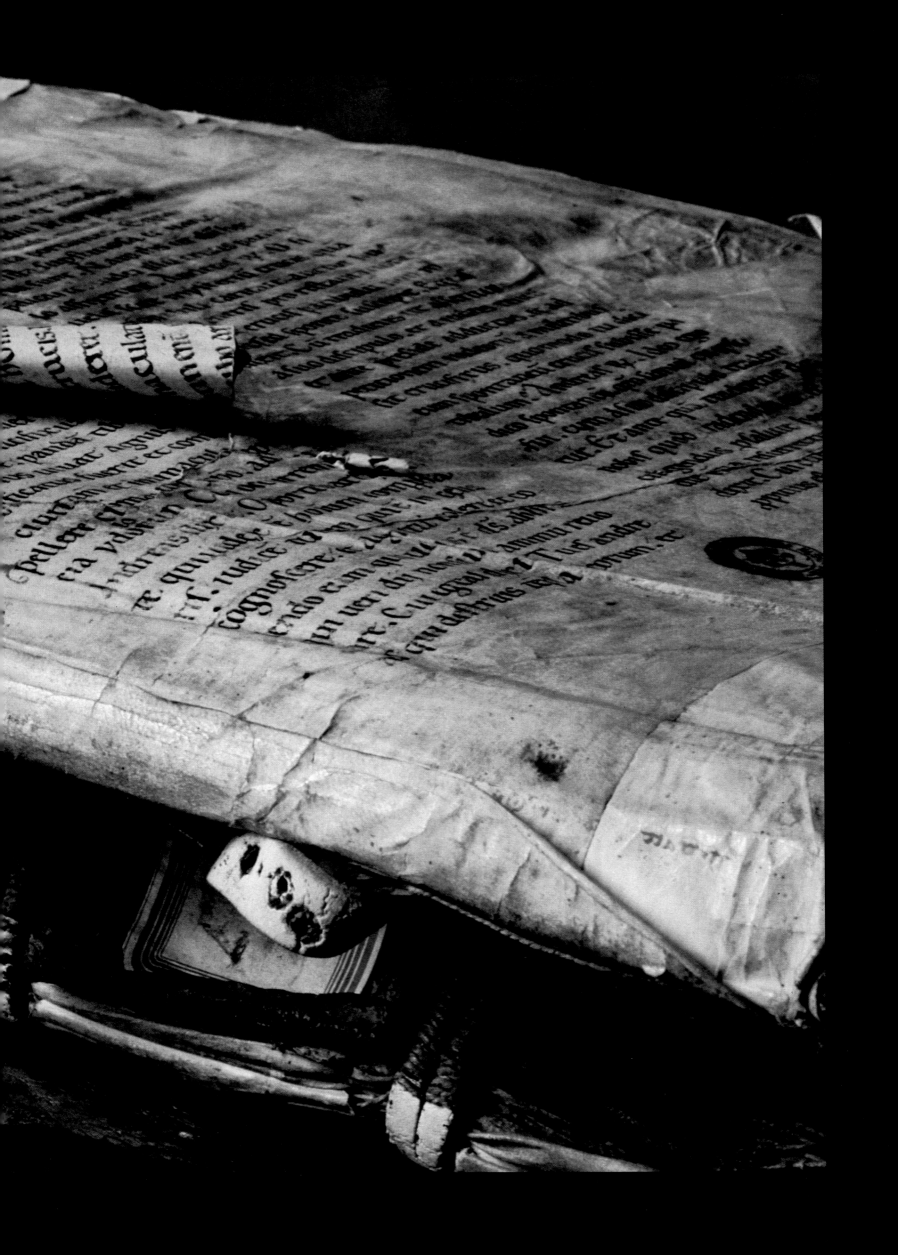

Papal Elections

Raimondo Manzini

'*Extra omnes!*' 'Everyone out!' As the shadows of twilight fall, the peremptory order of the Conclave Marshal rings out in the rooms adjoining the area of the Vatican in which the conclave is about to begin. The cardinals, vested in violet, have just entered the Sistine Chapel in procession while the hymn *Veni, Creator Spiritus,* ('Come, Creator Spirit') is sung. They come from the Pauline Chapel, where the Cardinal Chamberlain has celebrated the Mass of the Holy Spirit, in the course of which they received Holy Communion from his hands and listened to his sermon exhorting them to reach an early agreement on the name of the Pope-elect and to 'choose the one who is most worthy of the honour'.

In the Pauline Chapel, constructed in 1538 to the design of Sangallo by order of Pope Paul III, the strong and balanced architectural lines would have led their gaze towards the immense frescoes in which Michelangelo depicted the conversion of Saint Paul. There, blinded by light on the road to Damascus, his horse tumbling to the ground under the brightness of the heavenly vision, the future Apostle is shown stricken by the victorious Christ. Opposite this composition, on the other wall, would have been the *Martyrdom of Saint Peter*, also by Michelangelo. Now, facing the assembled cardinals, stands the same artist's titanic fresco *The Last Judgement*, where Christ has returned, raising his hand towards the just and the doomed, while from the vaults above, Michelangelo's powerful figures of patriarchs and prophets keep vigil over the holiness of the sanctuary.

'*Extra omnes!*' 'Everyone out!' Eighteen days have passed since the Cardinal Chamberlain solemnly declared, 'Yes, the Pope is dead'. During the *sede vacante*, the Cardinal Chamberlain substitutes for the Pope, though he is limited in his role to the day-to-day administration of the Church, assisted by a committee of three cardinals and by the daily general assembly of the College of Cardinals. From the moment that the Pope is declared dead, all papal officials cease to hold office, beginning with the Cardinal Secretary of State: seals are placed on all the rooms of the papal apartments, even on his furniture and library. Keys are removed from locked cabinets and the 'fisherman's ring', the personal seal of the Pontiff, is broken. All authority passes to the College of Cardinals, who now see to the ordinary running of the Church, beginning with the arrangements for the funeral of the dead Pope and for the conclave. However, they have absolutely no authority in any area which is exclusively the province of the Pope. Any decision taken in such an area is liable to be annulled by the new Pontiff. During the *sede vacante*, the College of Cardinals may not modify, annul or change any of the laws made by previous Popes concerning the order of the conclave or any other canonical matter concerning the rights of the Pope. The absolute primacy of Peter's jurisdiction must be safeguarded against any attempt to interfere with it, either internally by the Church or externally by civil authorities.

'*Extra omnes!*' 'Everyone out!' In the weeks that have passed since the death, Masses in memory of the Pope, the so-called *Novendiali*, have been celebrated in Saint Peter's basilica for nine days. At each Mass, the officiating cardinal delivers a eulogy on the dead Pope, his qualities and his achievements. According to the rules of the constitution of the conclave, cardinals now hurry to Rome from Churches scattered throughout the world to take part in the election of the successor. In the past, such a journey was often a problem, on occasions even adventurous and eventful: there are cases of cardinals who died as a result of travel fatigue. Everything is easier now, due to modern communications, but as late as 1914 and 1922, the cardinals of North and South America could not arrive by sea in time for the conclaves that elected the successors to Pius X and Benedict XV. For this reason Pius XI lengthened the waiting time from ten to fifteen days and Pius XII to eighteen days. Today, modern ships and supersonic aircraft bring the members of the Church's senate to Rome from the farthest ends of the earth. The universality as well as the unity of the Church is made manifest in such a gathering of cardinals, praying together in the Sistine Chapel.

'*Extra omnes!*' 'Everyone out!' The Cardinal Chamberlain, assisted by the Marshal of Sacred Ceremonies, now oversees the closing from the inside of all access to the conclave quarters, while the Prefect of the Sacred Palace and the governor of Vatican City, assisted by the Chief of the Swiss Guard, fulfil the same task from the outside. The echoes of bolts and of the great keys that lock the ancient doors ring out; the knocking of doors and windows breaks the silence, as all the openings facing outside the Apostolic Palace are sealed: for the very word, 'conclave', from the Latin *cum clave*, means 'closed by key'. Telephone lines are cut, except for the Chamberlain's telephone, which may be only used for urgent messages or for medical emergencies. All recording and transmitting equipment is banned. Silence and secrecy—these are the conditions imposed on all the cardinals and their assistants by a triple solemn oath. In the conclave, one voice above all must be heard: the voice of God, the voice of the Holy Spirit, which is to inspire the election according to the saying heard in the most recent conclave: 'The cardinals have elected you, but it is God who has chosen you!'

'*Extra omnes!*' 'Everyone out!' The shadows of twilight become darker: in the silent Sistine Chapel they watch and pray. The conclave has started.

Most of the early successors of Saint Peter, the first Bishop of Rome, were saints and martyrs. Emerging from the catacombs, where a new people, reborn of the Gospel, was to be the heir of pagan Rome, they came to be elected in an enforced, persecuted secrecy, while already the scattered little churches in Asia and Africa owed obedience to them as Bishops of Rome. Until the fourth century, the Popes were appointed by those little praying communities of deacons, priests and faithful, along with nearby bishops, but already they enjoyed an extensive and unquestioned authority. So when the edict of the Emperor Constantine enabled the Church to function openly and 'Peter' to take his seat at the Lateran, the widespread power of the Roman Pontificate had already been established and the primacy of Peter over all other churches, as instituted by Jesus Christ himself, was acknowledged everywhere.

The Christian Emperors, however, came into conflict with the power of the Church, for they attempted to extend their own authority over the internal affairs of the Church into the election of the Popes themselves. Moreover, they claimed the right to ratify even doctrinal and purely disciplinary decrees, even though the Church was not remiss in according them due honour and respect. This accentuated the need to safeguard the conduct of papal elections from such interference.

Eventually the Western Empire crumbled and finally fell in 476, when Odoacer deposed the last of the Caesars, Romulus Augustulus: soon Italy became a mosaic of Romano-Barbaric kingdoms. But when the Roman Emperor himself moved to Constantinople, capital of the Eastern Empire, he left to the Pope the overall civil charge of the Italian peninsula.

Good times alternated with bad. The Popes had to endure the interference of the barbarian kings on Italian territory; they also had to put up with the Byzantine Emperor at Constantinople, who wanted to be considered as the 'bishop from outside' and insisted on ratifying the election of Popes (for which privilege they even had to pay him a tax!). When a new Pope was elected, he could not be consecrated until the imperial permission arrived—and this was sometimes months *en route*. Constantine even wanted to preside over the Ecumenical Councils. In Italy, the Pope was subject to the whims of barbarian kings: when Pope Saint John I died in 526, the successor whom he had appointed was condemned by King Theodoric to die in prison because he would not allow the establishment of Arian worship in the East. (However, for the sake of peace and after the death of Theodoric, the papal candidate, Felix

IV, was elected.) In similar manner, the Byzantine Emperors forced the election of two Popes of their own choosing—Virgilius (537) and Pelagius (556)—and claimed for Byzantium 'parity of honour' with Rome.

In the years of the High Middle Ages, as the Teutonic and Roman cultures fused, the issue between the Church and Emperor became that of 'investitures'. The Popes refused to allow the Emperors and other feudal lords, greedy to possess episcopal and monastic property, to receive ecclesiastical appointments. Where such 'investitures' had occurred, they resulted in the shocking worldliness and the profanation of religious life. Over this state of corruption rose an outstanding figure, the monk Hildebrand, subsequently Pope Gregory VII, who formally established the distinction between the two powers—sacred and secular—and delineated their respective boundaries, giving pride of place to the spiritual. It was he who, still a monk, suggested to Pope Nicholas II in 1060 a number of strict regulations for the conduct of papal elections. During that century only the prelates in Rome itself had taken part in the elections. Tumultuously welcomed by the people of Rome itself the procedure had dissatisfied and disgruntled the German Emperors.

The exile of the Popes at Avignon in the fourteenth century arose from a difficult situation. For the previous century, the Popes had been obliged to live in other Italian cities because of the impossibility of governing Rome, which had become a dangerous theatre of bloody riots and violence. But worse was to follow. In the forty years of the Popes' residence in the Provençal city under the protection of the French court, further civil disorder, rebellion and pillaging took place in Rome, which prompted the people to appeal for the return of Peter to his See. The heroic initiative of Catherine of Siena (d.1380) brought the anxious Gregory XI back to the city, but further conflict was to ensue. When Gregory died, his successors were opposed by a succession of four anti-popes—Clement VII (1378–94) and Benedict XIII (1394–1417), elected at Avignon, and Alexander V (1409–10) and John XXIII (1410–15), elected at Pisa. This great schism of the West lasted until 1417, when it was ended by the Council of Constance.

With the twilight of the Middle Ages and the dawn of the Renaissance came the fragmentation of the spiritual and cultural unity of the West—that unity which had managed to absorb the barbarians and had been immortalised in the great cathedrals. Papal elections became the object of continuing human and worldly rivalries as new secular powers attempted to interfere with them. Conclaves lengthened, continuing for months on end. (The vacancy left by the death of Nicholas IV in 1292 lasted for two years and three months!) Even when the choice of successor had been made, it often caused uproar among the people. Abuse and corruption set in. Laxity and self-indulgence seemed to hold sway among the lords and princes while society was rife with plots of barbaric cruelty.

Major events in human history involved the Church as well. In 1453 the Eastern Empire fell and with the capture of Constantinople by Mahomet the Great, the thousand-year-old Christian-Byzantine civilisation perished. Thirty-nine years later came the discovery of America by Christopher Columbus, a sea captain sponsored by the Spanish Catholic kings, Ferdinand and Isabella, who further extended their influence when they took Granada, thereby capturing the last Moslem kingdom in Western Europe. In 1520 Luther broke the bonds of his communion with Rome. On 13 December 1545 the first session of the Council of Trent opened the Catholic reform known to history as the Counter-Reformation. Thereafter in the sixteenth century, great saintly figures and new religious orders signal the exuberant renascence of Catholicism in full communion with Peter. The golden years of faith begin.

But in the nineteenth century, the sudden Napoleonic invasion saw Rome occupied and Pius VII imprisoned and deported; the same troubled century saw the Vatican's loss of Rome and all other temporal power. Such events persuaded Popes Pius VI, VII and IX successively to pass legislation protecting the freedom of the conclave from any assault or physical violence. Indeed, such was the real fear of external assault that when Pius VII died, the election was held at the Quirinal Palace because of its defensible position on a hill in the city of Rome. During the reign of Pius IX (1846–78), the temporal power of the Popes came to an end and, with the establishment of the new Italian government in Rome, the Holy Father retreated to the Vatican Palace on the other side of the Tiber. The conclave that elected Leo XIII in 1878 took place in the Sistine Chapel, as have all conclaves since then.

The history of electoral legislation is worth telling, for the Popes themselves have devoted so much attention to passing the strictest laws governing the process of succession.

'The first of the legal acts to free the Church,' writes Daniel Rops of the Académie Française in the third volume of his monumental *History*, 'was passed under the pontificate of the energetic Pope Nicholas II (1059–61), who had been elected at the instigation of the monk Hildebrand, the future Gregory VII. This put an end to the choice of Pope by the Emperor.'

'We have decided,' says this text of historic importance, 'that at the death of the sovereign Pontiff of Rome and of the universal Church, the cardinal bishops will take the utmost care over the question of a successor. Then they will consult the cardinal clerics, the rest of the clergy and the people in order to obtain their agreement to a new election. . . . They should give preference in their choice to someone from the Roman Church, if a suitable candidate can be found there; otherwise, they should choose someone from another Church, while maintaining due honour and reverence to Henry, the present King, the future Emperor.'

Originally, the cardinals were the Roman clergy. They were divided into three categories: the *presbyters* or priests of the twenty-five 'titles' or quasi-parochial churches of Rome (in the beginning, under persecution, these 'churches' had been the homes of Christians and the 'titles' were the names of their owners—when the persecutions ceased, the churches proper were built and the 'title' of each became that of a saint or martyr); the *deacons*, responsible for the administration of church property in the thirteen zones of the city; and the *seven bishops of the 'suburbicarian' dioceses*, i.e., the dioceses that encircle Rome itself: Ostia, Albano, Frascati, Palestrina, Porto and Santa Rufina, Sabina and Poggio Mirteto, Velletri. All these 'cardinals' were the first papal counsellors and assistants.

Initially, the cardinals all lived in Rome and the surrounding dioceses. But slowly the Popes began to nominate prelates living outside Rome and even outside Italy. In the thirteenth to the fifteenth centuries the total number of cardinals did not normally exceed thirty. Pope Sixtus V, in 1586, fixed the maximum number of the Sacred College at seventy. This number was slightly exceeded by John XXIII in 1958, but Paul VI brought the number up to 143. It was John XXIII who decided that all the cardinals should also be bishops. (Until the last century, some had been deacons, not even priests, like Pius IX's Secretary of State, Antonelli.)

It was Pope Alexander III who, in 1179, extended to all the cardinals and to them alone the right to elect a Pope, on condition that the person elected acquired at least two-thirds of the votes cast. But in 1274, circumstances forced Gregory X to promulgate in the course of the Council of Lyons a new Constitution, *Ubi Periculum*, containing even stricter legislation, most of it inspired by the canon law of his day. The reasons for doing so are to be found in the story of the conclaves that took place earlier in that century.

When the division among the cardinals after the death of Pope Innocent III (1216) became unreasonably prolonged, the citizens of Perugia forced them into an enclosure and even restricted their food and water until the election of Pope Honorius ended the conclave. Similarly, at the death of Gregory IX (22 August 1241), the Romans shut up the cardinals in the vaults of Septimius Severus, on the slopes of the Palatine Hill. The same happened again later when, following the death of Clement IV (29 November 1268), the members of the Sacred College gathered in the papal palace at Viterbo. After the conclave had remained deadlocked for eighteen months, the local townspeople, apparently on the advice of Saint Bonaventure and with the aid of the army chief, Alberto of Montebuono, shut up the cardinals in the papal palace and proceeded to deprive them not only of bread and water but also of the palace roof, which they proceeded to remove. The episode is rightly famous. A compromise was reached and Pope Gregory X elected in 1271.

The Constitution *Ubi Periculum* of that Pope was therefore intended to avoid similar disorders in the future. According to its provisions, when the Pope dies, the cardinals should wait ten days for the arrival of their colleagues at the conclave. Each might have a single assistant, a priest or layman. The meeting was to take place if possible wherever the Pope died, otherwise in the bishop's palace or similar location in a nearby city. There they would gather in a single room, without dividing walls or curtains, and lead a communal life, apart from free access to one reserved room. These two apartments were to be closed so securely that no one could enter or leave without being observed; no one could talk to another cardinal except publicly and with the permission of the Sacred College. No messages, letters or goods might be admitted. The keys of the conclave were to be guarded: the internal keys by the Cardinal Chamberlain, the external by the Marshal of the Conclave. Provisions were to be brought in through a carefully guarded revolving window and were to be examined for illegal letters and packets. If after three days the cardinals had been unable to reach agreement, they could have a single dish for lunch and another for supper; after five days, they were to be limited to bread, wine and water. Prayer, silence and listening for the word of God were to prevail.

The exact and strict regulations of Gregory X had the effect of limiting the conclave that nominated Innocent V to a single day. But because of the premature deaths of four Popes in two years (1276–7—Gregory X, Innocent V, Adrian V and John XXI), three conclaves had been required: the new discipline proved too much for the cardinals to bear and they abrogated it (*Licet* of 30 September 1276).

Back to square one! The elections began to lengthen once more: six months for the conclave of Nicholas III (25 November 1277), six months for Martin IV (22 February 1281), ten months for the election of Nicholas IV (22 February 1288). At the death of this Pope, the Apostolic See remained vacant for two years and three months.

Pope Celestine V, in his pontificate of only five months, reviewed the regulations and restored the laws of Gregory in three Bulls, *Quia in Futurum* of 28 September 1294, *Pridem* of 27 October 1294 and *Constitutionem* of 10 December 1294. These gave clearer directives on the manner of electing a new Pope, offering three possible forms which are still in force today: by *inspiration* (the Pope being acclaimed by the public proposal of one or more cardinals); by *compromise* (following an elaborate method of mediation between two or more parties); and by *scrutiny* (a secret ballot requiring a voting majority of two-thirds). The last procedure is the most common.

In 1562, with the Constitution *In Eligendis*, signed by all the cardinals of the time, Pius IV decided that the conclave should not possess funds other than those strictly necessary to meet the expenses of its own deliberations and those of the previous Pope's funeral, with the sum fixed at 1,000 ducats. No longer should the conclave be held responsible for paying any debts left by the previous Pope. Such measures were evidently intended to avoid the danger of simony. Pius IV also decreed that the cells for the cardinals should be decided by drawing lots and the conclave placed under strict surveillance.

It was in 1621 that Gregory XV intervened with new legislation in *Aeterni Patris*, which banned the compilation of the so-called 'black and white lists'. This index divided the cardinals into those condemned to exclusion from consideration and those favoured with inclusion among the *papabili*: this had been a privilege going back to the influence of Charlemagne, who, as 'protector of the Church', claimed the right of Christian potentates to 'intercede' for one candidate and veto another. Thus in 1590, Philip II of Spain, son of Emperor Charles V, abandoning his father's discretion in these matters, made a heavy-handed intervention in the conclave by presenting a list of no less than fifty 'excluded' cardinals and another of seven 'favoured' cardinals—all of them Spanish!

In the light of this intervention, it is important to cite the conclave which put an end to the exercise of this claimed right: that of August 1903, which saw the election of the saintly Pope Pius X. The first votes favoured Cardinal Rampolla, but the Emperor of Austria, Franz Joseph, considered him too 'italianising' and francophile; having vetoed Rampolla, he nominated Cardinal Puzjna, the archbishop of Cracow. The cardinals were enraged and protested strongly. Nevertheless, the votes slipped away from Rampolla and went to Cardinal Sarto; when he ascended the *cathedra* on 20 January 1904, he promulgated the Constitution *Commissio Nobis*, in which he utterly abolished the use of the veto, under pain of excommunication, thus re-establishing, after six centuries, the absolute freedom of papal elections from all such external interference.

In our own century, after the *Vacante Apostolicae Sedis* of Pius XII and John XXIII's *motu proprio*, Pope Paul VI completely overhauled the existing legislation with the Constitution *Romano Pontifice Eligendo* of 1975.

The novel measure that attracted the greatest interest was that also introduced by Pope Paul VI in his *motu proprio, Ingravescentem Aetatem*, concerning the age-limit on the electors of a new Pope. Since 1970, this law has applied to all cardinals, even those newly appointed who had not yet received the distinctive red biretta. The Constitution of Pope Paul lays down that cardinals who 'at the time that a conclave starts have already completed their eightieth year of age' lose the right to take part in the election. In addition, the Constitution fixed the maximum number of cardinal electors at 120.

However, Pope Paul's Constitution made no changes in the traditional method of conducting the election itself. If a majority is not obtained, the voting must be repeated, morning and afternoon, for as the Constitution clearly states: 'Immediately after one ballot in which no election is made, the cardinal electors shall proceed at once to a second in which they cast a new vote'. Should the voting proceed for three days without agreement, it is suspended for a maximum of twenty-four hours to allow a break for prayer, free discussion and a brief exhortation from the chief Cardinal Deacon. Then the voting recommences. After another seven ballots, if the required majority has not been reached, a further pause for prayer, discussion and exhortation takes place. The conclave may then continue to a further seven ballots.

When the election has been duly made in accord with the legal requirements, the Cardinal Deacon or the eldest cardinal seeks the consent of the elected prelate in these words: 'Do you accept your canonical election as Supreme Pontiff?' Having received the consent, the Deacon asks, 'By what name do you wish to be called?'

For most of papal history, the change of name has been intended to denote the detachment of the Pope from his previous life: the practice is based on the symbolic change which Jesus himself made to the name of Simon the fisherman: 'You are Peter and on this rock I will build my Church.' The change of name became established in 533, when Mercury, a priest of the Roman basilica of San Clemente, considered that it was disrespectful to be a successor of Peter while bearing the name of a pagan god. Thus he entered the Papacy as Pope John II.

A famous nineteenth-century historian and author of an important *Apologia for Christianity*, Luigi Vittorio Emilio Bougaud (1824–88), made the observation that in the hierarchical structure of the Church and its government are found all three of the juridico–institutional forms that have developed in history for the political ordering of human society: the democratic, the oligarchic and the monarchic.

Democracy is represented in the structure of the Church in that the humblest lay person can, via the priesthood, episcopate and cardinalate, ascend to the highest ecclesiastical office. *Oligarchy* is seen in the College of Cardinals, who alone have the right to elect the Pope and have a privileged place in the government of the Church (where the bishops also have a share with the Pope under the principle of *collegiality* and within its limits). Finally, *monarchy* is practised by the Pope, since he continues the apostolic succession and exercises an absolute right over the whole Church, for on him alone Jesus has conferred the authority to guard and proclaim the Gospel message: 'You are Peter and on this rock I will build my Church; Feed my lambs, feed my sheep.'

The analogy of Bougaud, ingenious as it is, fails to express the full character and profound meaning of the Church's hierarchical organisation, for that structure is of divine provenance. It was Jesus himself who laid the basis for this structure when he instituted first the twelve and then the seventy, his apostles and his disciples. At the summit stands Peter, who possesses a complete, supreme and universal jurisdiction over the whole Church.

This authority comes from God and it is God who confers it: 'you have not chosen me, I have chosen you'. So the Pope appoints the bishops and the bishops ordain priests, but all these answer a call, a vocation that only God can give. The authority of the Church must be powerful but it must above all be one of service, after the example of Christ himself, who said: 'He who wishes to be first among you, let him be the last.'

The following is a list giving the length of conclaves from Gregory X's Constitution of 1274 to today:

Innocent V	Arezzo 1276	1 day
Adrian V	Rome 1276	18 days
John XXI	Viterbo 1276	20 days
Nicholas III	Viterbo 1277	6 months
Martin IV	Viterbo 1280–81	6 months

(one cardinal died during this conclave, another two were kidnapped!)

Honorius IV	Perugia 1285	5 days
Nicholas IV	Rome 1288	10 months
Celestine V	Rome, Rieti, Anagni and Rome again, 1292–94	
		27 months
Boniface VIII	Naples 1294	1 day
Benedict XI	Perugia 1303	1 day
Clement V	Perugia 1305	11 months
John XXII	Carpentras 1314–16	2 years, 14 days
Benedict XII	Avignon 1334	6 days
Clement VI	Avignon 1342	13 days
Innocent VI	Avignon 1352	12 days
Urban V	Avignon 1362	$1\frac{1}{2}$ months
Gregory XI	Avignon 1370	1 day
Urban VI	Rome 1378	2 days
Boniface IX	Rome 1389	$1\frac{1}{2}$ months
Innocent VII	Rome 1404	1 week
Gregory XII	Rome 1406	12 days
Martin V	Constance 1417	(elected by the Council)
Eugene IV	Rome 1431	3 days
Nicholas V	Rome 1447	2 days
Callistus III	Rome 1455	4 days
Pius II	Rome 1458	9 days
Paul II	Rome 1464	1 day
Sixtus IV	Rome 1471	3 days
Innocent VIII	Rome 1484	8 days
Alexander VI	Rome 1492	4 days
Pius III	Rome 1503	6 days
Julius II	Rome 1503	a few hours
Leo X	Rome 1513	1 week
Adrian VI	Rome 1521–22	13 days
Clement VII	Rome 1523	50 days
Paul III	Rome 1534	2 days
Julius III	Rome 1549–1550	2 months and 10 days
Marcellus II	Rome 1555	6 days
Paul IV	Rome 1555	12 days
Pius IV	Rome 1559	4 months
Pius V	Rome 1565–66	17 days
Gregory XIII	Rome 1572	2 days
Sixtus V	Rome 1585	4 days
Urban VII	Rome 1590	8 days
Gregory XIV	Rome 1590	2 months
Innocent IX	Rome 1591	1 day
Clement VIII	Rome 1592	20 days
Leo XI	Rome 1605	18 days
Paul V	Rome 1605	18 days
Gregory XV	Rome 1621	2 days
Urban VIII	Rome 1623	18 days
Innocent X	Rome 1644	1 month and 16 days
Alexander VII	Rome 1655	50 days
Clement IX	Rome 1667	18 days
Clement X	Rome 1670	4 months
Innocent XI	Rome 1676	2 months
Alexander VIII	Rome 1689	1 month and 21 days
Innocent XII	Rome 1691	5 months
Clement XI	Rome 1700	52 days
Innocent XIII	Rome 1721	1 month
Benedict XIII	Rome 1724	2 months and 12 days
Clement XII	Rome 1730	over 4 months
Benedict XIV	Rome 1740	6 months
Clement XIII	Rome 1758	52 days
Clement XIV	Rome 1769	2 months and 4 days
Pius VI	Rome 1775	over 4 months
Pius VII	Venice 1799–1800	$3\frac{1}{2}$ months

Leo XII	Rome 1823	26 days	
Pius VIII	Rome 1829	over 1 month	
Gregory XVI	Rome 1831	54 days	
Pius IX	Rome 1846	a little over 2 days	
Leo XIII	Rome 1878	$1\frac{1}{2}$ days	
Pius X	Rome 1903	4 days	
Benedict XV	Rome 1914	3 days	
Pius XI	Rome 1922	4 days	
Pius XII	Rome 1939	1 day	
John XXIII	Rome 1958	3 days	
Paul VI	Rome 1963	3 days	
John Paul I	Rome, August 1978	1 day	
John Paul II	Rome, October 1978	2 days	

134 The afternoon sun throws the shadow of the dome of Saint Peter's on to the Apostolic Palace and the area behind it. On 6 August 1978, Pope Paul VI died in Castelgandolfo, in the sixteenth year of his reign. Only a few weeks later, on 29 September, his successor, John Paul I, was found dead in his bed.

135–136 On a simple catafalque beneath the cupola of Saint Peter's, the mortal remains of Paul VI lie in state in front of the Confessio. Thousands of people pay their last respects, while the Swiss Guard and those who worked closely with the dead Pope keep watch.

137–138 The Church and the world bid farewell to Pope Paul VI with a Requiem Mass on the Square in front of Saint Peter's. The cardinals sit in a row before the entrance to the basilica, and later they move up to the altar, in front of which the unadorned coffin of light cypress wood stands on a carpet. Behind the cardinals are representatives of world governments and, in the foreground, representatives of other churches and the world episcopate.

139–140 Extra Omnes: after invoking the Holy Spirit, the Cardinal Chamberlain shows all those not participating in the election of the Pope out of the conclave. Only the actual proceedings of the election take place in the Sistine Chapel. The cardinals spend the time between each of the ballots in rather makeshift quarters behind sealed doors, cut off from the rest of the world.

141–142 Bianco o Nero? White or black smoke? That is the question which the thousands of expectant onlookers ask each other. Nor, for over half an hour, can the millions watching on TV be certain whether a Pope has been elected or not.

143–144 Habemus Papam! We have a Pope: Albino Luciani. A short time after Cardinal Felice's announcement, the newly-elected Pope appears on the balcony, greeted by great rejoicing. His chosen name, John Paul I, commemorates both of his immediate predecessors.

145–152 Kings and statesmen from all over the world attend the inauguration ceremony of the new Pope. Among them are the German chancellor, Helmut Schmidt; the Argentinian dictator, General Videla; Prince Rainier and Princess Grace of Monaco; the Italian prime minister, Andreotti; the Prince and Princess of Liechtenstein, and the King and Queen of Spain.

153 John Paul I, desiring simplicity, dispensed with the tiara, the papal triple crown. Only the Pallium, a piece of woollen cloth worn across his shoulders, identifies him as Bishop of Rome. One hundred and twenty priests stand by to distribute the consecrated Host to the congregation, during the Eucharistic ceremonies celebrated by the new Pope.

154–157 On the day of his inauguration Mass, the new Pope receives heads of state and delegations in the Sala Regia. Among them are the American vice-president, Walter Mondale,

Madame Giscard d'Estaing, wife of the president of France, prime minister Andreotti of Italy, the Canadian prime minister, Pierre Trudeau and chancellor Schmidt of the Federal Republic of Germany.

158 The smiling, humble parish priest, Don Albino Luciani, who, via the small diocese of Veneto and the Patriarchy of Venice, was, for one short month, head of the Vatican. Yet in this short time, he succeeded in becoming a folk-hero. Cardinal Deacon Confalonieri compared Pope John Paul I to a comet which unexpectedly lights up the sky and as quickly disappears, but nevertheless leaves people stunned and shaken. The short period of office of this man with the happy eyes and steady faith built a bridge to the next pontificate.

159 In October, the ritual connected with the papal vacancy and the conclave commences anew. The election of the Archbishop of Cracow, Cardinal Wojtyla, who, in his own words, came from a distant country, is a great surprise. He is the first non-Italian to be elected Pope in 450 years and the first Pole in the history of the Papacy. This Pope, too, with his open, direct manner, communicates spontaneously with people. He brings to the Papacy a more robust character and, with his unique unaffectedness, will bring about many changes in the Vatican.

160–161 In the unique setting of Saint Peter's Square, around 200,000 people take part in the inauguration of Pope John Paul II. The ceremonies take a long time, as the Pope insists on exchanging a few words with each of the cardinals who come to pay their respects, even with Cardinal Pignedoli, who was considered a favourite for the succession. At the end of the Mass, the Pope throws all protocol aside and, under the disapproving eyes of the officials, walks straight into the delighted crowd.

162–163 In a special audience, Pope Wojtyla receives some 12,000 Roman nuns, among whom is a group of nuns from twenty-six enclosed order convents, attending a papal audience for the first time. Their delight and exuberance do not seem to perturb the Pope in any way.

164–165 In November 1978, John Paul II officially takes over the Basilica of Saint John Lateran, the cathedral of the See of Rome. For the first time, he takes his place on the throne of the Bishop of Rome, surrounded by the Vicar for Rome, Cardinal Poletti, and the bishops. Before the tabernacle, which contains relics of the apostles SS. Peter and Paul, the Pope celebrates Mass as Bishop of Rome.

166–167 The Pope is no longer the 'Prisoner of the Vatican', as he was a hundred years ago, when Italian troops occupied Rome. He can now set out by helicopter from his own 'Heliport', be it to his summer residence at Castelgandolfo in the Albani mountains, or to Assisi on pilgrimage, or even to Fiumicino Airport on his way to places around the world.

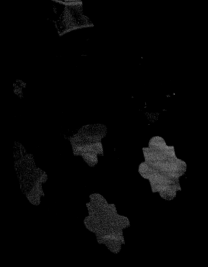

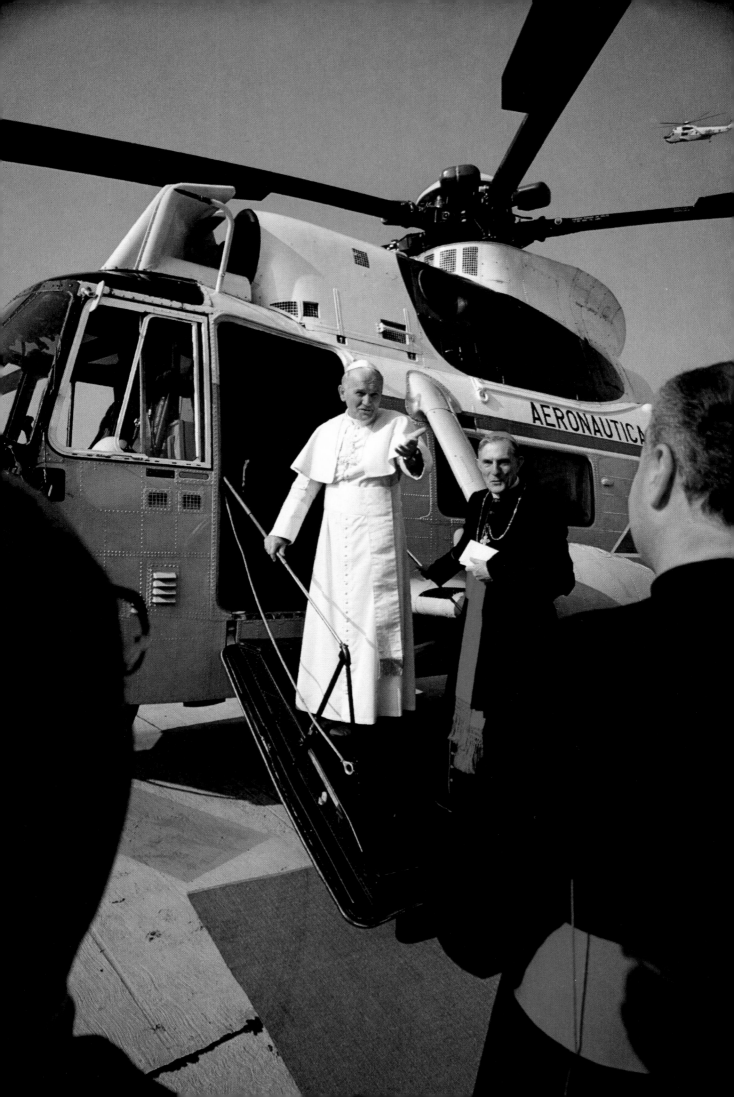

List of the Popes

The names of anti-popes are given in square brackets.

S. = saint; B. = blessed; M. = martyr.

1. S. Peter, M.	†64/67(?)
2. S. Linus, M.	67–76(?)
3. S. Anacletus or Cletus	79–90(?)
4. S. Clement, M.	92–101(?)
5. S. Evaristus, M.	99–107(?)
6. S. Alexander I, M.	107–116(?)
7. Sixtus I, M.	116–125(?)
8. S. Telesphorus, M.	125–136/38(?)
9. S. Hyginus, M.	136/38–140/42(?)
10. S. Pius I, M.	140/42–154/55(?)
11. S. Anicetus, M.	154/55–166(?)
12. S. Soter, M.	166–174(?)
13. S. Eleutherius, M.	174–189(?)
14. S. Victor I, M.	189–198/99(?)
15. S. Zephyrinus, M.	199–217(?)
16. S. Callistus I, M.	217–222
[S. Hyppolytus	217–235]
17. S. Urban I, M.	222–230
18. S. Pontian, M.	230–235
19. S. Anterus, M.	235–236
20. S. Fabian, M.	236–250
21. S. Cornelius, M.	251–253
[Novatian	251–258(?)]
22. S. Lucius I, M.	253–254
23. S. Stephen I, M.	254–257
24. S. Sixtus II, M.	257–258
25. S. Dionysius	259/60–267/68(?)
26. S. Felix I, M.	268/69–273/74(?)
27. S. Eutychian, M.	274/75–282/83(?)
28. S. Caius, M.	282/83–295/96
29. S. Marcellinus, M.	295/96–304
30. S. Marcellus I, M.	307–308(?)
31. S. Eusebius, M.	308/09/10
32. S. Melchiades	310/11–314(?)
33. S. Silvester I	314–335
34. S. Mark	336
35. S. Julius I	337–352
36. Liberius	352–366
[Felix II	355–358]
37. S. Damasus	366–384
[Ursicinus	366–367]
38. S. Siricius	384–399
39. S. Anastasius I	399–402
40. S. Innocent I	402–417
41. S. Zozimus	417–419

42. S. Boniface I	418–422
[Eulalius	418–419]
43. S. Celestine I	422–432
44. S. Sixtus III	432–440
45. S. Leo the Great	440–461
46. S. Hilary	461–468
47. S. Simplicius	468–483
48. S. Felix III (II)	483–492
49. S. Gelasius I	492–496
50. Anastasius II	496–498
51. S. Symmachus	498–514
[Lawrence	498–506]
52. S. Hormisdas	514–523
53. S. John I, M.	523–526
54. S. Felix IV (III)	526–530
55. Boniface II	530–532
56. Dioscorus	530
57. John II	533–535
58. S. Agapitus	535–536
59. S. Silverius, M.	536–537
60. Vigilius	537–555
61. Pelagius I	556–561
62. John III	561–574
63. Benedict I	575–579
64. Pelagius II	579–590
65. S. Gregory the Great	590–604
66. Sabinian	604–606
67. Boniface III	607
68. S. Boniface IV	608–615
69. S. Deusdedit I	615–618
70. Boniface V	619–625
71. Honorius I	625–638
72. Severinus	640
73. John IV	640–642
74. Theodore I	642–649
75. S. Martin I, M.	649–653
76. S. Eugene I	654–657
77. S. Vitalian	657–672
78. Deusdedit II	672–676
79. Donus	676–678
80. S. Agatho	678–681
81. S. Leo II	682–683
82. S. Benedict II	684–685
83. John V	685–686
84. Conon	686–687
[Theodore	687]
[Paschal	687]
85. S. Sergius I	687–701
86. John VI	701–705
87. John VII	705–707
88. Sisinnius	708
89. Constantine	708–715
90. S. Gregory II	715–731
91. S. Gregory III	731–741
92. S. Zachary	741–752
[Stephen II	752]
93. Stephen II (III)	752–757

94. S. Paul I	757–767
[Constantine	767–768]
[Philip	768]
95. Stephen III (IV)	768–772
96. Adrian I	772–795
97. S. Leo III	795–816
98. Stephen IV (V)	816–817
99. S. Paschal I	817–824
100. Eugene II	824–827
101. Valentine	827
102. Gregory IV	827–844
[John	844]
103. Sergius II	844–847
104. S. Leo IV	847–855
105. Benedict III	855–858
[Anastasius	855]
106. S. Nicholas the Great	858–867
107. Adrian II	867–872
108. John VIII	872–882
109. Marinus I	882–884
110. S. Adrian III	884–885
111. Stephen V (VI)	885–891
112. Formosus	891–896
113. Boniface VI	896
114. Stephen VI (VII)	896–897
115. Romanus	897
116. Theodore II	897
117. John IX	898–900
118. Benedict IV	900–903
119. Leo V	903
120. Christopher	903–904
121. Sergius III	904–911
122. Anastasius III	911–913
123. Landon	913–914
124. John X	914–928
125. Leo VI	928
126. Stephen VII (VIII)	928–931
127. John XI	931–935/36
128. Leo VII	936–939
129. Stephen VIII (IX)	939–942
130. Marinus II	942–946
131. Agapitus II	946–955
132. John XII	955–963
133. Leo VIII	963–964
134. Benedict V	964–965
135. John XIII	965–972
136. Benedict VI	973–974
137. Boniface VII	974, 984–985
138. Benedict VII	974–983
139. John XIV	983–984
140. John XV	985–996
141. Gregory V	996–999
[John XVI	997–998]
142. Silvester II	999–1003
143. John XVII	1003
144. John XVIII	1003/04–1009
145. Sergius IV	1009–1012

146. Benedict VIII	1012–1024	190. John XXI	1276–1277	241. Alexander VII	1655–1667
[Gregory (VI)	1012]	191. Nicholas III	1277–1280	242. Clement IX	1667–1669
147. John XIX	1024–1032	192. Martin IV	1281–1285	243. Clement X	1670–1676
148. Benedict IX	1032–1045	193. Honorius IV	1285–1287	244. B. Innocent XI	1676–1689
149. Sylvester III	1045–1046	194. Nicholas IV	1288–1292	245. Alexander VIII	1689–1691
150. Gregory VI	1045–1046	195. S. Celestine V	1294	246. Innocent XII	1691–1700
151. Clement II	1046–1047	196. Boniface VIII	1294–1303	247. Clement XI	1700–1721
152. Damasus II	1048	197. B. Benedict XI	1303–1304	248. Innocent XIII	1721–1724
153. S. Leo IX	1049–1054	198. Clement V	1305–1314	249. Benedict XIII	1724–1730
154. Victor II	1055–1057	199. John XXII	1316–1334	250. Clement XII	1730–1740
155. Stephen IX (X)	1057–1058	[Nicholas V	1328–1330]	251. Benedict XIV	1740–1758
156. Benedict X	1058–1059	200. Benedict XII	1334–1342	252. Clement XIII	1758–1769
157. Nicholas II	1059–1061	201. Clement VI	1342–1352	253. Clement XIV	1769–1774
158. Alexander II	1061–1073	202. Innocent VI	1352–1362	254. Pius VI	1775–1799
[Honorius II	1061–1064]	203. B. Urban V	1362–1370	255. Pius VII	1800–1823
159. S. Gregory VII	1073–1085	204. Gregory XI	1370–1378	256. Leo XII	1823–1829
[Clement III	1080–1098]	205. Urban VI	1378–1389	257. Pius VIII	1829–1830
160. B. Victor III	1086–1087	[Clement VII	1378–1394]	258. Gregory XVI	1831–1846
161. B. Urban II	1088–1099	206. Boniface IX	1389–1404	259. Pius IX	1846–1878
162. Paschal II	1099–1118	[Benedict XIII	1394–1417]	260. Leo XIII	1878–1903
[Theoderic	1100–1102]	207. Innocent VII	1404–1406	261. Pius X	1903–1914
[Albert	1100]	208. Gregory XII	1406–1415	262. Benedict XV	1914–1922
[Sylvester IV	1105–1111]	209. Alexander V	1409–1410	263. Pius XI	1922–1939
163. Gelasius II	1118–1119	[John XXIII	1410–1415]	264. Pius XII	1939–1958
[Gregory VIII	1118–1121]	210. Martin V	1417–1431	265. John XXIII	1958–1963
164. Callistus II	1119–1124	[Clement (VIII)	1423–1429]	266. Paul VI	1963–1978
165. Honorius II	1124–1130	211. Eugene IV	1431–1447	267. John Paul I	1978
[Celestine II	1124]	[Felix V	1439–1449]	268. John Paul II	1978–
166. Innocent II	1130–1143	212. Nicholas V	1447–1455		
167. Anacletus II	1130–1138	213. Callistus III	1455–1458		
[Victor IV	1138]	214. Pius II	1458–1464		
168. Celestine II	1143–1144	215. Paul II	1464–1471		
169. Lucius II	1144–1145	216. Sixtus IV	1471–1484		
170. B. Eugene III	1145–1153	217. Innocent VIII	1484–1492		
171. Anastasius IV	1153–1154	218. Alexander VI	1492–1503		
172. Adrian IV	1154–1159	219. Pius III	1503		
173. Alexander III	1159–1181	220. Julius II	1503–1513		
[Victor IV	1159–1164]	221. Leo X	1513–1521		
[Paschal III	1164–1168]	222. Adrian VI	1522–1523		
[Callistus III	1168–1178]	223. Clement VII	1523–1534		
[Innocent III	1179–1180]	224. Paul III	1534–1549		
174. Lucius III	1181–1185	225. Julius III	1550–1555		
175. Urban III	1185–1187	226. Marcellus II	1555		
176. Gregory VIII	1187	227. Paul IV	1555–1559		
177. Clement III	1187–1191	228. Pius IV	1559–1565		
178. Celestine III	1191–1198	229. S. Pius V	1566–1572		
179. Innocent III	1198–1216	230. Gregory XIII	1572–1585		
180. Honorius III	1216–1227	231. Sixtus V	1585–1590		
181. Gregory IX	1227–1241	232. Urban VII	1590		
182. Celestine IV	1241	233. Gregory XIV	1590–1591		
183. Innocent IV	1243–1254	234. Innocent IX	1591		
184. Alexander IV	1254–1261	235. Clement VIII	1592–1605		
185. Urban IV	1261–1264	236. Leo XI	1605		
186. Clement IV	1265–1268	237. Paul V	1605–1621		
187. B. Gregory X	1271–1276	238. Gregory XV	1621–1623		
188. B. Innocent V	1276	239. Urban VIII	1623–1644		
189. Adrian V	1276	240. Innocent X	1644–1655		

Vatican City

1. Bronze Door
2. Steps of Pius IX
3. Scala Regia
4. Scala Nobile
5. Loggias
6. Cortile di San Domaso
7. Tower of Nicholas V
8. Cortile del Maggiordomo
9. Cortile di Sisto V
10. Cortile del Triangolo
11. Cortile del Maresciallo
12. Cortile dei Pappagalli
13. Cortile Borgia
14. Cortile della Sentinella
15. Sistine Chapel
16. Borgia Tower
17. Appartmento Borgia
    Raphael Rooms
    (2nd Floor)
18. Cortile di Belvedere
19. Apostolic Library (Salon
    of Sixtus V)
20. Apostolic Library
    (Museo Sacro)
    Map Gallery
    (2nd Floor)
21. Galleria Lapidaria
22. Library Courtyard
23. Tower of the Winds
24. New Wing of the
    Chiaramonte Museum
25. Chiaramonte Museum
26. Cortile della Pigna
27. Apostolic Library (Museo
    Profano)
    Galleria dei Candelabri e
    degli Arazzi
    (2nd Floor)
28. I Quatro Cancelli
29. Museo Gregoriano Egizio
    Museo Gregoriano Etrusco
    (2nd Floor)
30. Pio-Clementine Museum
31. Cortile Ottagono
32. Bramante Steps
33. Fontana della Galera
34. Cortile delle Corazze
35. Entrance to the Vatican
    Museums
36. Gregoriano-Profano
    Museums Pio-Christiano,
    Missionario
37. Art Gallery
38. Porta di Sant'Anna
39. Chiesa di Sant'Anna
40. Patrimony of the Holy
    Father
41. Courtyard of the Swiss
    Guard
42. Via di Belvedere
43. Tipografia Poliglotta
    Vaticana
44. Via del Pellegrino
45. Restoration Workshops for
    Tapestries
46. Printing House for
    L'Osservatore Romano
47. Headquarters of the
    Security Services
48. Main Post Office
49. Via della Tipografia
50. Palazzo del Belvedere
51. Via della Posta
52. Via Pio X
53. Statue of St Andrew
    (Entrance to Grottoes)
54. Fontana del Sacramento
55. Stradone dei Giardini
56. Casina di Pio IV
57. Viale del Giardino
    quadrato
58. Fontana dell'Aquilone
59. Viale centrale del Bosco
60. Headquarters of Vatican
    Radio
61. Lourdes Grotto
    St John's Tower
62. Ethopian Seminary
63. Viale del Seminario
    Etiopico
64. Viale Marconi
65. Railway Station
66. Mosaic School
67. Viale dell'Osservatorio
68. Palazzo del Governatorato
69. Via del Governatorato
70. Via delle Fondamenta
71. Chiesa di S. Stafano
72. Largo di S. Stefano
73. Pallazzo del Tribunale
74. Residenza dell'Arcipreta
75. Palazzo S. Carlo
76. Piazza Santa Marta
77. Ospizio di Santa Marta
78. Parish House and Sacristy
    of St Peter
79. Entrance to the
    Vatican Grottoes
80. Square of the Roman
    Martyrs
81. German College
82. Ingresso 'Arco delle
    Campane'
83. New Papal Audience Hall
84. Palace of the Sanctum
    Officium, Headquarters of
    the Congregation for the
    Doctrine of the Faith
85. Post Office
86. Information Office
87. Piazza Sant'Uffizio

Plan Scala, Florence.
Distributed in Italy by Ufficio
Pellegrini e Turisti del Vaticano,
Rome. Reproduced by kind
permission of Ufficio Pellegrini e
Turisti del Vaticano, Rome.

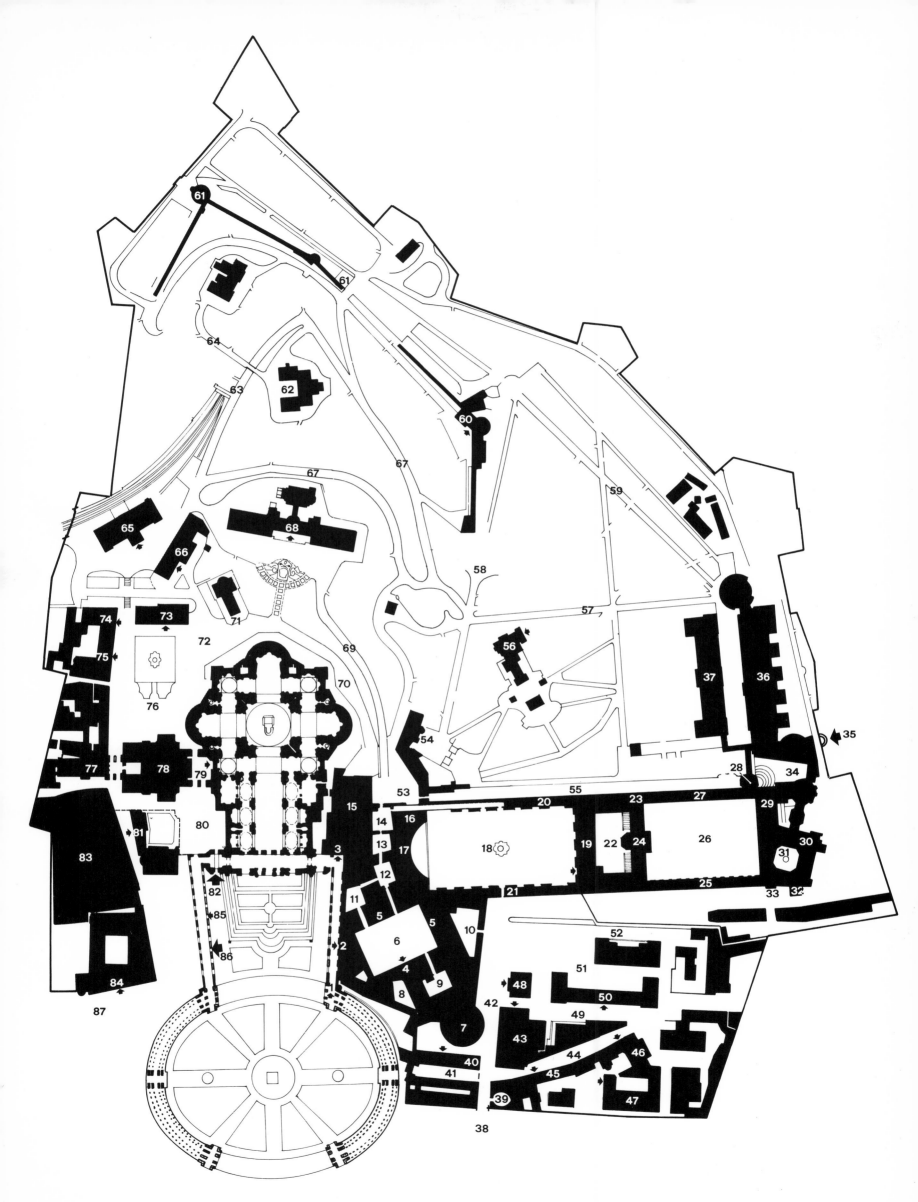

Postscript

This book on the Vatican makes no attempt to be complete in any way. It shows pictured moments. I am convinced that many things that are written about and photographed in the Vatican by tourists—and perhaps also by experts—are mere fragments. There is so much that simply cannot be photographed, or is hidden. And bureaucracy doesn't help much either. To photograph the Vatican station, for example, I had to procure three written permits: one was for the station itself; but, because a train happened to be in the station when I went to take the pictures, I was obliged to get another permit, this time to photograph the station with a train standing in it. However, when I arrived in the station, two weeks later, permits in hand, the train was being loaded with freight, which necessitated a further permit. The permit had to be applied for in writing and took twenty-four hours to be issued. But a train stops in the station at most once a week. . . .

To take the photographs for this book, I spent over 160 days in Rome. The fact that I managed to get the whole work finished at all is mainly thanks to Mrs Marjorie Weeke, Padre Karl-Heinz Hoffmann and Bishop Andrea Deskur, from the Pontificia commissione per le comunicazione sociale, who were a great help and gave me the will to keep going when I wanted to give up. Now that the book is finished and printed, I think it was well worth the effort.

Most tourists in Rome manage to spend only a short time in the Vatican and, on the whole, don't have the opportunity to experience any of the important events and ceremonies. I hope that this book will help them remember what they did see and give them a glimpse of what they didn't; I also hope that it will offer an incentive and a taste of things to come to those who have yet to experience the Vatican.

For these pictures, I used Pentax cameras with lenses ranging from Fish-Eye to 1000 mm telephoto and everything in between. For daylight shots, I used Kodachrome film 64 ASA, and for indoor shots and those in artificial light, Ektachrome film 400 ASA, rated as 800 ASA in development.

My special thanks are due to Theodor Wieser for his great help in editing the photo captions.

Fred Mayer